READY
SET
Grow!

D1235592

READY SET GROW!

MARK JACKSON

REGULAR BAPTIST PRESS
1300 North Meacham Road
Schaumburg, Illinois 60173–4888

Library of Congress Cataloging-in-Publication Data

Jackson, Mark, 1928–
    Ready, set, grow! : a faith and practice primer for
    Regular Baptists / Mark Jackson.
          p.   cm.
    Includes bibliographical references
    ISBN 0–87227–138–2
    1. Regular Baptists—Doctrines. 2. Baptists—Doctrines.
    I. Title
BX6389.37.J28 1989   89–38819
286'.13—dc20   CIP

CONTENTS

This study book of Christian doctrine
is dedicated to my father,
DR. PAUL R. JACKSON.
Promoted to Glory in 1969,
he would have appreciated this effort
whether it was good or worthless.
He was that kind of dad!

PREFACE

I n the desperately darkening days of deepening apostasy as revealed by the spiraling plunge of theological conviction in our so-called Christian America, we witness a parallel declension in the true church. Sadly, even good churches are affected by the downward slide. We may be more Biblical in our beliefs than the apostate, but the awful softening process is already underway. Furthermore, we are becoming more and more content with less and less in the areas of convictions, standards, separation and commitment on the part of our local members.

The material for this study course was originally prepared with the growing realization that many who seek membership in our churches urgently need instruction in the great doctrines of the Word of God and in the unusual but Biblical character and polity of our church government. Furthermore, as the request for small-group study material has increased, I felt that this was another field in which such doctrinally and practically oriented material could prove helpful.

Whether used as Bible study material, Sunday School lessons or membership instruction, this book is designed to strengthen the more mature saint in his faith and to instruct the blessed "babes in Christ." It will also provide, for that vast host of believer-Christians in between these two points, a wealth of practical material that somehow—in the happy rush-hours of their conversion and the busy crunch of hectic church life—they may have missed altogether!

It has been my experience that great numbers of otherwise reasonably well-grounded believers have not been exposed to some of the practical matters in the operation of a church. Therefore, I have written some of these chapters with this observation in mind.

Recognizing that many folk are being saved and added to the church and that many people come from other churches that are not grounded in the particular persuasion of us Baptists, I have given these chapters a good sprinkling of materials designed to underscore our convictions as being Baptists as well as being Christians. We are distinctive and our people need to know it.

The selected Bible doctrines to which we have given consideration are important to a balanced view of spiritual life. There are obviously many other equally important doctrines. You will want some additional books to aid in your study. A list of helpful books appears at the end of this book. You may wish to add them to your personal library.

It is my prayer that the study of these brief lessons will result in more church members, better church members and solid Baptist church members!

—*Dr. Mark Jackson*
Schaumburg, Illinois

THE DOCTRINE OF SALVATION

When the average person hears the word "theology," he throws up his mental hands, turns off and checks out because he assumes that anything under that subject is either dry or unintelligible. However, the word simply means "the doctrine of God." It is a composite of two Greek words: *theos* meaning "God" and *logos* meaning "the doctrine" or "the Word." Therefore, all theology is instruction about God, His Word, His plans and His Being. Not only is it *not* dry, it is thrilling! Every believer should fill his heart and mind with the great doctrine of theology.

At the very moment a person comes to Christ and is born again, many things transpire. We may be aware only that we are saved from sin and its awful consequences, but the Bible indicates that several things happen simultaneously with that event. We will look at four.

Preachers use the word "soteriology" to describe the comprehensive term "salvation." It, too, is a composite word: *soter* means "savior," which comes from the Greek word *sodso*, "to save"; *logos* means "the doctrine/the Word, or to relate in systematic discourse, or the teaching." Reduced to an intelligible sentence, soteriology is *the teaching about salvation.*

We want to briefly examine several important Bible doctrines we call soteriological truths: conversion, justification, regeneration and glorification.

Before we can properly proceed, we must make sure we

understand the basis for our Christian hope. The crucial matter of our personal relationship to God must be clearly understood. Without a perfect understanding and a firm assurance of a satisfactory condition existing between a sinner and a holy God, there is little need to study the truths about salvation.

Think your way through these questions and references:

1. What is man's natural condition?

    2 Corinthians 4:4

    John 3:18

    Ephesians 2:1, 2

    Romans 3:23

2. What is God's provision for this desperate plight of man?

    John 3:16

    John 5:24

3. Through what means has God provided salvation?

    Romans 3:24–26

4. Who will be saved?

    John 1:12

    Romans 10:13

5. How is one saved?

    Acts 16:31

    John 6:37

    Acts 17:30

    Romans 10:9, 10

Conversion

Definition

By conversion we mean *the voluntary change in the mind of the sinner, in which he turns from sin to Christ.*

Scripture

Acts 17:3.

Truths Involved in Conversion

There are two factors involved in the conversion of an individual.

Negatively

There is REPENTANCE, the turning from sin (Acts 2:38).

Positively

There is FAITH, the turning to Christ (Heb. 11:6).

A great deal of confusion exists today about what constitutes conversion. Many people are told if they just "believe on Jesus," they will go to Heaven when they die. We refer to this as "easy believism" and believe it is insufficient to redeem the soul. It is our conviction that along with an adequate faith that Jesus Christ is the Son of God, that He died and shed His blood for our sins and rose for our justification, we must also have a genuine sorrow and repentance for sin.

Being sorry for sin does not save you. However, one great evidence of faith having been truly born in your heart is a turning in repentance from sinful ways that were part of your life prior to conversion.

Regeneration

Definition

An easy-to-remember definition is that regeneration is *a spiritual change in the spirit of man wrought by the Spirit of God.*

Scripture

John 1:12.

"To regenerate" indicates an original condition or generation that was ultimately undone, that now through regeneration is restored. God created a lovely arrangement in the Garden of Eden. He placed a perfect man and a perfect woman into a perfect setting. That original generation was created to enjoy God and bring glory to Him.

Sin ruined the man and the setting. From then until now all men have been born in sin, and the deadly stain of sin and its long-range results have been the awful consequences.

God, Whose love for His creatures and creation never diminished, immediately instituted promises and plans to restore the creature and creation through regeneration (Gen. 3:15). He ultimately sent His Son to pay the redemptive price of death for sin (Rom. 3:23), thus making a way for sinful men to once again walk with God.

There are other Scriptural terms that are similar to "regeneration":

New birth—John 3:3–7

Spiritual quickening—John 5:21

New nature—2 Peter 1:4

"Regeneration" should not be confused with either of the following:

Baptism—It is not a means of regeneration but rather a testimony of our relationship with Christ in His death, burial and resurrection.

Reformation—Doing good deeds, attempting to obey the Law and being a good neighbor are insufficient to redeem or regenerate the soul.

Questions for Study

1. What does the word "theology" mean?

2. Why do men need to be saved?

3. From memory write out John 3:16, check it against the Bible and correct it for any mistakes. Repeat this process until you can write the verse word perfect.

4. What are the two elements involved in conversion to Christ?

5. Memorize Romans 10:9, 10 and John 5:24.

THE DOCTRINE OF SALVATION

It would be impossible to assign a numerical order of importance to the doctrines of salvation since they are all crucial to the whole. Without any one of them our redemption would be incomplete. However, if one does stand out from the others, it is justification.

The question of how sinful man can be just before God is the most important issue that faces man. It has been asked from the beginning of time (Job 9:2). Some insist that man's justification before God is all of God's *grace;* others feel it is brought to pass by man's good *works;* and others contend it is a mixture of *grace and works* (Eph. 2:8, 9).

The importance of arriving at a proper conclusion should be self-evident, for improper interpretation of the Scriptures here will lead to faulty conclusions in other doctrinal areas.

Justification

Definition

Justification is *a judicial act of God by which, on account of Christ, the sinner is declared to be no longer exposed to the penalty of sin but is restored to favor with God.*

This is the legal aspect of salvation. A holy God sits at the bar of eternal justice and declares all men to be sinners, guilty and condemned. Then, on account of Christ's finished work on our behalf (Rom. 5:8), God declares Himself to be legally satisfied and marks our account "Paid in Full." Thus we are restored to His favor, and our legal status is changed from one of guilt and condemnation to that of forgiveness and acceptance.

Scripture

Romans 3:24 and 5:21.

Truths Involved in Justification

Forgiveness of Sin

Romans 8:1 declares there is "no condemnation [judgment] to them which are in Christ Jesus," and Romans 3:24 says we are "justified freely by his grace." The word "freely" is the same word used in John 15:25 that is translated "without a cause"; that is, without anything on our account that deserved it.

Note the definition again. In justification, God does not declare the sinner innocent. This is impossible, for we *are* sinners. But in *grace* He does declare us justified and forgiven. We are no longer exposed to penalty on the legal ground that the penalty has already been borne by Christ to Whom we are united by faith. This is the legal procedure of acquittal (2 Cor. 5:21).

The acquittal process of human government will allow no penalties to be executed, but neither will it provide any rewards. It is merely the setting free of the formerly guilty. However, when God justifies (acquits, sets free), He also, in grace, provides *restoration, approval, promotion* and *promise.*

Imputation of Christ's Righteousness

Second Corinthians 5:20 and Romans 4:3–6 indicate that we are to be reconciled to God. This involves a restoration to God's favor from a once-broken fellowship. Imputation is the glorious truth that we guilty, Hell-bound sinners have been clothed with Christ's own righteousness and that God sees us as He sees His own Son—holy, spotless, righteous and pure. This unmerited, unmeritable, ill-merited favor is pure grace!

This is one of the most blessed truths in the Bible. It also may be the most difficult for new believers to comprehend! God looks upon us now with total favor and sees us as being as perfect and without sin as His own holy Son! This fact is beyond our feeble ability to fathom.

Some lengthy meditation on the wonders of the imputation of Christ's righteousness to unworthy sinners will result in a proper humility and a determination to please Him.

Sanctification

Definition

"Sanctification is the separation and dedication of a person or object to and for God, to belong wholly to Him and to be used for His glory" (Emery H. Bancroft, *Christian Theology, Systematic and Biblical*, Rev. ed., [Grand Rapids: Zondervan, 1949], p. 243).

Scripture

Hebrews 10:10, 14.

The basic meaning of sanctification is *separation*. It

involves being set apart in holiness unto God.

In the Old Testament certain people, places or things were sanctified for special service before God. Specific items were sanctified for use in worship, and a person could not use them for mundane purposes without coming under judgment. They were holy unto God. These people and things were separated from secular usage and dedicated solely to God.

In the New Testament we learn that since we are the peculiar possession of Christ and the temple of the Holy Spirit (1 Cor. 3:16), we are set apart or separated unto God for special purposes. We call this sanctification.

It is a wonderful thing to be chosen of God to be separated out of all creation to be special before Him. Our daily lives should evidence this truth of salvation.

Various Steps in Sanctification

Positional—Begins at Conversion

Hebrews 10:10; Ephesians 1:6 and 1 Corinthians 6:11. These verses teach us that at the moment of salvation we are separated or set apart to God once for all. We call this *positional sanctification*. This is the declarative aspect of sanctification, which—closely related to justification—places us by divine decree into Christ and into the *position* that we hold before God. It is in this *position* that God sees us as He sees His Son, with all the holy perfections pertaining to that relationship and union.

At this point it is also necessary to understand the difference between the indwelling and the filling of the Holy Spirit.

Every believer—at the same moment he is saved—becomes the permanent tabernacle of the Holy Spirit

(1 Cor. 12:13; Heb. 13:5). Thus we are indwelt by the Holy Spirit.

Ephesians 5:18 indicates that after the Spirit comes in to dwell, a continuous filling for refreshing and empowering is also needed. Many have fallen into the error of believing that the filling of the Spirit is some "super" event having special relationship to a post-salvation experience. The charismatic movement of our present day, with its unbiblical emphasis on speaking in tongues and other "signs," should be studiously avoided as a shallow and improper interpretation of the filling of the Holy Spirit. The difference between the indwelling and filling of the Holy Spirit needs to be clear in the believer's mind. Indwelling is instantaneous and permanent; filling is continuous and dependent upon our submission to Christ.

Progressive—Continues throughout Life on Earth

Second Corinthians 3:18; 2 Peter 3:18. While our salvation relationship to Christ is permanently secured and divinely assured through justification and regeneration, and while we are *positionally* set apart in a holy and perfect relationship to Almighty God, there is a distinct sense in which we are to "grow" in grace and knowledge. We may call this *practical* or *progressive sanctification*.

We need to recognize the gulf between what we are and what we ought to be spiritually. It is in this area that there should be spiritual growth and progress. We are to be "... [being] changed into the same image" (2 Cor. 3:18) step by step. The spiritual transforming process goes on as we mature in Christ.

How is this "perfecting" accomplished?

1. By faith—a faith that appropriates the Person of Christ (1 Cor. 1:30).

2. By constant study of the Word (John 17:17).
3. By judging self and sin and seeking personal holiness (Rom. 6:19; 2 Cor. 7:1).
4. By consciously yielding to our Father (Heb. 12:9, 11).

Permanent—Will Be Complete at the Return of Christ

First Thessalonians 3:13. A sinless perfectionism that some think to be possible through certain efforts in our spiritual lives or the idea of the eradication of the old nature at the time of conversion is unfortunately wishful thinking. Honest men admit, as Paul did in Romans 7:15–25, that there is a constant war in us between the flesh and the Spirit.

Romans 8:21–23 describes the yet-to-come release from this sinful "bondage of corruption" when our *bodies* are to be redeemed. When we are ushered into His presence, we shall be perfect in every way. We call this *permanent sanctification*.

Positional sanctification and permanent sanctification are like railroad tracks in a picture that converge in the distance. Positional—what we are declared to be by a gracious and loving God; permanent—what we will ultimately be in the day we are ushered into His presence. When these two merge at the Rapture, we shall be like Him, perfected in His image.

Conclusion

These four main subjects that we have considered under *soteriological truths* are but a few of the things that transpire at the moment of salvation. They are each necessary and equally important. They should be understood and mastered by every believer. These truths are hidden to the eyes of unbelievers and all too often to the casual eyes of the careless believer.

Questions for Study

1. Memorize the definition of justification.

2. Ask two or three of the deacons of your church to give you their definitions of justification.

3. Can man in any way be justified by his works? Have you read Ephesians 2:8 and 9?

4. Choose a friend who is a believer and attempt to explain to him the imputation of Christ's righteousness.

5. On a scale of one to ten, how far have you grown in understanding the grace of God in saving you?

6. When will we believers reach perfection?

7. Are you a saint?

Chapter 3

THE DOCTRINE OF INSPIRATION

The importance of the doctrine of the inspiration of the Bible cannot be overestimated. It is the epicenter of all Christian theology and is a field of doctrine that must be held and defended at all costs. The satanic attack upon God's Word and its authority began in the Garden of Eden when the Devil first asked, "Yea, hath God said?" The attack has not changed in its insidiousness or its tactics, for the Devil has continued to cast aspersions upon the authority, trustworthiness and infallibility of the Word of God.

Views of Inspiration

Definition

By inspiration we mean that the original manuscripts were given by the Holy Spirit of God to godly men and that He controlled the very words and language of Scripture, providing for us a perfect and complete revelation of His mind and of Himself.

Scripture

Psalm 119:89; 2 Timothy 3:16 and 2 Peter 1:21 offer Scriptural evidence of inspiration. The Scriptures are a "God-breathed" book, which is the meaning of the words in the 2 Timothy reference. This means that when men turn to the Bible, they turn to a book that speaks with the authority of God for all matters both doctrinal and practical.

Two words most commonly define the kind of inspiration to which we refer: "verbal" and "plenary." By "verbal" we mean that the very words of the Bible were given by God to men; by "plenary" we mean that all the words—the Bible in its entirety—were equally inspired by God.

Liberal View

The common viewpoint of the liberal is that the Bible contains the Word of God. Our position is that it does not merely contain the Word of God but *is* the Word of God. The liberal scholar gives himself the right to determine what part is and what part is not inspired. However, we simply accept that all its parts and statements are the very Word of God.

One can readily see how our judgment could be colored relative to the matter of interpretation. If we were to judge which parts were inspired, it would be easy to declare any part with which we did not agree as uninspired.

Neoevangelical View

The neoevangelical, while claiming an evangelical approach to the Bible, would have reservations about the subject of inspiration as herein defined.

Fundamentalist View

We believe that the original manuscripts as they came from "holy men of old" were absolutely inspired and that every word they wrote was a part of the infallible record God intended we should have. While we do not have copies of the original writings, archaeology and such finds as the Dead Sea Scrolls and the Mardikh Tablets in Syria have given us volumes of evidence that our present copy is a highly trustworthy and authoritative edition. We do not claim infallibility for our King James Version of the Bible. However, we believe that since it has been God's intention to preserve truth for us and since godly men have given their lives to maintain its accuracy, we have in hand a fully trustworthy text of the inspired Word of God.

It has been said of the two Testaments, "In the Old, the New is concealed; in the New, the Old is revealed." Thus the important linkage between the two Testaments becomes plain.

The Bible is a wonderful revelation of God. The following three steps help us focus on this revelation.

Revelation Is Possible

If an omnipotent God exists, He can communicate in any way He chooses.

Revelation Is Probable

Since God can communicate and since He is love, it is logical and probable that He would reveal Himself.

Revelation Is Necessary

If man is the helpless man that he finds himself to be and that the Bible declares him to be, a divine revelation is necessary to help him find a way out of his dilemma.

We believe that a gracious God has revealed Himself and that an inspired Bible was His method.

God can also be identified through nature (Rom. 1:18), divine providential dealings, history and the Person of Jesus Christ. But it remains for the Bible, an impregnable fortress of truth, to be the full and ultimate revelation of the Person of God.

Some invariably ask how we can be sure that our

version represents the original manuscripts, thus reflecting as perfectly as possible the inspired revelation.

For many years the revelation was oral. Genesis 15:1 states, "The word of the LORD came to Abram. . . ." Then the Spirit of God began to move upon holy men, causing them to write in inspired fashion. It is a small step from the time the apostles wrote the New Testament to the time the early church fathers of the second and third centuries began to use and quote the Scriptures frequently.

The fourth century saw three major translations: The Codex Sinaiticus, now in Russia; the Codex Vaticanus in Rome; and the Codex Alexandrinus in London. Such translations carry us quickly to the 1600s when our King James Version was translated.

The Old Testament, written between 1500 B.C. and 400 B.C., became a library of books about the time of Ezra and Nehemiah after the Babylonian captivity. The attitude of Christ toward them caused the early church to accept them as God's Word. For many centuries and only after careful scrutiny and tests, the Church has accepted as canonical the sixty-six books of the Bible as the Word of God.

A word about the apocryphal books should be included here. We do not believe they are part of the canon of Scripture for the following reasons:

1. They were never a part of the Jewish Scriptures.
2. They were not written in Hebrew.
3. They were not quoted by Christ or the apostles.
4. For the first four centuries after Christ, they were not included in any catalog of canonical writings.
5. They were not included in Scripture by anybody until the church of Rome arbitrarily added them at the Council of Trent in the sixteenth century.

6. They contain inaccuracies in history and contradictions in doctrine.

The problem of "What version?" is an increasing problem today because new editions, translations and paraphrases appear regularly. As I said earlier, we do not claim infallibility for the King James Version (translated in 1611), but we do believe that the Lord has protected His Word and that we have a trustworthy version that leaves no doubts concerning our doctrinal convictions. In the course of 375 years, some words have become archaic. The New King James Bible has attempted to bring some of the outmoded words into modern terminology and is a fine translation.

Another recommended translation is the American Standard Version (ASV), translated in 1901. It, too, has been revised with upgraded word changes. It is now called the New American Standard Bible (NASB). The New International Version (NIV) is also widely acclaimed as a good translation. Even these good translations have their faults, and one should be careful not to be dogmatic over the issue of versions. Other translations and paraphrases run the gamut from the Living Bible to the Cotton Patch version! Far too many of them are produced by either liberal or otherwise questionable scholarship. Often in their attempt to make the Bible "readable," the editors have used unacceptable texts or have been more concerned about style and readability than about inspiration and textual accuracy.

We do not recommend the Revised Standard Version or the Living Bible. Although popularly received, the RSV had some biased translators who rejected the deity of Christ, and their bias shows through in places. The Living Bible is *not* a translation but rather a paraphrase and is not intended to convey the actual and accurate sense of the original manuscripts. So, although it makes easy reading, it is not a faithful translation of the original language. The very popular Good News for Modern Man has serious problems and is not recommended.

One of the oldest and strongest arguments for the trustworthiness of the Bible is its amazing unity in the midst of diversity. By this we mean that, in spite of the multitudinous and diverse circumstances under which the Bible was produced, it still has an amazing characteristic— a unity that pervades the content of the book.

It is sometimes said that the Bible contains contradictions, or that the Bible and science do not agree. Neither is true. Any assumed contradiction can be satisfactorily resolved by careful research, and at no point does the Bible disagree with science, nor true science with the Bible. Problems occur when all scientific data is unavailable on a given subject or where full revelation of the Bible is unavailable to the student.

You may confidently rest on this fact: when science has all its information in hand and the Bible truth is fully revealed, they will agree perfectly. Such is our confidence in the God Who gave us the Bible. He and His Word are infallible. The Bible is not intended to be a book of geography, history or science; but when it speaks on any subject, it is infallible. Any seeming discrepancy between the Bible and science can be put down as a failure of science to have all the necessary facts in hand or in our failure to have all necessary revelation at hand!

For instance, only in recent years has medicine known the importance of the blood as it relates to life. George Washington, our first president, was literally bled to death by doctors who believed that bloodletting would restore health. Now we know that he needed blood, and if they had given it to him rather than drained it out of him, he might have lived for many more years! The Bible, however, states in Leviticus that the "life of the flesh is in the blood"—a fact that God knew long before scientists discovered it. If all the facts—spiritual and scientific—had been available or revealed, early medicine surely would have been different!

The Wonders of Biblical Construction

The Diversity of Writers

Nearly forty men from a wide diversity of walks of life were engaged by the Holy Spirit in the writing of the Bible. There were poets, princes, fishermen, herdsmen, doctors, musicians, poor men, rich men, learned men and unlearned men. In fact, every grade of culture and class of society was represented by the Bible writers. But, in spite of this diversity, there is an amazing unity in the Scriptural content.

The Diversity of Time

The writing of the Scriptures covered approximately sixteen hundred years, during which the Bible writers were separated from each other by geography and by differing customs of their lands. Considering the amazing changes that transpire in just a single lifetime, one can only begin to imagine the difficulty of trying to put together a Bible under false pretenses and with the problem of the diversity of time.

The Diversity of Circumstances

Parts of the Bible were produced while their writers were in prisons; others, while they were in palaces. Some of the writers were in deserts; some were in the city; some were in captivity; some were in exile; and some dwelt as free men in their own lands. But in every instance, the blessed unity of the Scriptures is seen.

The Diversity of Language

At least three different languages were used in the writing of the Bible—Hebrew, Aramaic and Greek. When we consider the peculiarity of expressions and idioms that pertain to different languages, we recognize the difficulty of the diversity of language.

The Diversity of Literary Forms

Every conceivable literary form is found in the Bible. The stories of Genesis are unequaled for beauty and attraction; Job is unrivaled for drama; Ruth, unparalleled for romance; Proverbs, unmatched for ethics; Ecclesiastes, profound in its philosophy. The hymns, poetry, logic, prophecy, biography and letters of the Scriptures give us an enormously wide comprehensive literary form, making the marvel of the Bible that much more a miracle.

The Diversity of Appeal

The Bible has an appeal to all men: the scientist, the philosopher, the rich, the poor, the wise and the unlearned. It speaks the universal language of men—the language of their lost condition and a hope for their depraved souls.

What a wonderful Book a blessed God has given to His creatures as a revelation of Himself, His plans, our needs and His divine intervention to meet those needs.

Questions for Study

1. Are there any contradictions in the Bible?

2. Do we have any of the original Bible manuscripts available to us today?

3. Ask your teacher or pastor the value of such recent archaeological discoveries as the Dead Sea Scrolls.

4. Does the Bible claim to be the Word of God? Where?

5. Is the King James Version of the Bible inspired, or is it a translation from an inspired original text?

6. Can you trust the Bible to be accurate on any subject?

7. Is the Apocrypha a legitimate part of the Bible?

8. How many writers did the Holy Spirit employ in the production of the Scriptures?

Chapter 4

PRACTICAL THEOLOGY

You will not find a chapter or paragraph heading "Practical Theology" in theology books, for it may not properly fall within the scope of theological discourse. You will find, however, that all the textbook theology you can cram into your head will be relatively useless unless sanctified with some practical application and down-to-earth implementation. Even in this, the Bible is the source of knowledge in making faith a day-to-day practical thing, changing our lives from self-centered to Christ-centered.

The book of Philippians is the greatest of textbooks in "the practicalities." Note the following verses from that book:

1:10	Choose the best way.
1:10	Live without offense.
1:27	Reflect the gospel in your manner of life.
1:28	Do not be afraid of enemies.
1:29	Suffer for Christ.
4:5	Be moderate in all things.
4:8	Think on pure and lovely things.
4:19	Trust the Lord to supply your needs.

Read Philippians and underline the scores of practical commands and suggestions it contains. The above are merely brief samples. You will find this little four-chapter book to be most helpful to your Christian walk. Familiarize yourself with it.

There are four things worthy of careful consideration when you give thought to the essentials that should characterize your daily life.

The Christian's Walk

It is important to learn early in our Christian experience that our lives are to be lived in such a way as to glorify God. Therefore, every day should be a challenge to live gloriously for Christ. To do this there are four things to practice daily that will ensure growth and spiritual stability:

The Importance of the Word

An often quoted phrase is desperately true: "This Book will keep you from sin, or sin will keep you from this Book." Scripturally, Psalm 119 declares many things about the importance of the Word:

Verse	9	Provides cleansing power
	11	Protects from sin
	41	Provides salvation
	42	Gives answers for the critics
	67	Keeps us from going astray
	70	Keeps us in spiritual 'condition'
	72	Is better than gold
	105	Provides light for difficult paths
	130	Gives understanding

It is essential that a personal commitment to regularly read and cheerfully obey the Word of God be made in every Christian life.

The Importance of Prayer

Our personal, daily contact with the Lord in prayer is a vital part of spiritual growth. John 14:13, 14 and 15:16 give some interesting sidelights into the value of prayer.

Furthermore, prayerlessness is sin (1 Sam. 12:23). Establish some time every day when you can read and pray. You will find rich reward in doing so.

The Importance of Fellowship

We are told in Hebrews 10:25 not to forsake the gathering "of ourselves together, as the manner of some is . . . *and so much the more* [as we come to the end of the age]."

Forsaking spiritual fellowship in the Lord's house can be fatal to spiritual vitality—*initially*, because any failure to obey God's command brings us under His corrective hand; and *practically*, because there is a direct relationship between spirituality and faithfulness to the Lord's house. There certainly are exceptions (shut-ins and the like); on the other hand, some who come to church regularly are hypocrites and some are carnal. But the general rule still stands: spirituality and faithfulness in church service go hand in hand.

The Importance of Witnessing

"I will make you fishers of men," said the Lord. The Great Commission of Matthew 28:19, 20 and the gospel appeal of Mark 16:15 lay stress upon the man-to-man approach in getting the gospel out. It is interesting and instructive to note that the early disciples went out two by two, and the present church has *no better technique given to it*. It is an observable fact that the church with an aggressive visitation ministry and soul-winning program will see God's blessing and growth.

The Christian's Warfare

Our battle is fourfold, and we need to remember that it is a constant battle. The moment we let down, the enemies will come in like a flood. Note these four conspiring foes: Satan and company (Eph. 6:11, 12; James 4:7); the apostasy (Jude 1:3, 4); the world system (1 John 2:15 and 5:4); carnality (Rom. 8:7, 8).

The Bible description of the Christian life is one of soldiering and battle. Some people have a misconception that being a Christian solves all problems and removes any struggles with sin and self. The Scriptures clarify that Satan is a living foe, that the world-system, sponsored by the Devil, categorically opposes spiritual growth, and that the flesh is intrinsically evil.

With this revelation before us, it is important that we use the resources in the Word of God to defeat our foes and live victoriously.

The Christian's Responsibility

Upon our becoming Christians, certain responsibilities become ours. It is not sufficient to be a pew-warmer, sharing nothing of the burden of reaching a world for Christ or of using God-given talents to glorify His name.

Part of our new relationship is planning for a life of ministry for Christ and understanding that often even good things need to be laid aside as we reevaluate our priorities. It is important that we develop a love for the brethren (even unlovely ones!) and pray for a willingness to "suffer" all things for Christ's sake.

The possibility of full-time ministry should be given serious consideration. Ask the Lord what He would have you do. He may have some wonderful plans in store for you that you wouldn't want to miss.

A whole reestablishment of priorities becomes necessary as we seek to live for Christ. We must get involved in a Sunday School class, develop some new Christian friends and make church a central part of our lives.

The Christian's Stewardship

Stewardship is simply the recognition that we are totally *His;* that is, everything we are, have and hope to have is *His* to do with as He desires. Our strength, our time, our minds, our energy, our wealth—they all are *His.*

The Bible teaches that it is our responsibility to be faithful stewards (1 Cor. 4:2). Therefore, whether stewardship of time or money, we should constantly remember that we will be called upon to give an account to the Lord in a day not too far ahead (2 Cor. 5:10).

Stewardship is frequently referred to in the realm of money. We must not fail to understand what the Bible teaches us about this highly practical matter.

While the Old Testament teaches that the tithe belongs to the Lord, the New Testament teaches proportionate giving (1 Cor. 16:1, 2). It is our conviction that the tithe should be a basic minimum in determining our responsibility to the Lord in the matter of giving. *Shall we do less under grace than that which was required by law?*

Since the church is God's designed institution for this age, we firmly believe that the tithe—and above that, offerings— belong to the Lord *through the local church.* Often people wish to invest in spiritual programs outside the church, and we believe that individuals desiring to do so should make such gifts real offerings above and beyond their tithing. The Bible speaks of "tithes *and offerings,*" seeming to differentiate between the two.

And since so many people ask . . . yes, I believe that you should determine your tithe according to your gross income and not after taxes! The principle of liberality as described in Luke 6:38 should not be forgotten in planning our giving.

So keep your stewardship a matter of believer-obedience and lay your gifts before Him. Remember that since the tithe is the Lord's, you have no right to determine where it should go—it is the Lord's. Also, remember that you have not begun to *give* until after you have given your tithe!

A little deeper spirituality reminds us that *all* we have is His anyway and that when we learn to get along on less and return more to Him, we have learned some of the greater lessons of the spiritual life.

Questions for Study

1. What are your greatest resources in defeating sin in your life?

2. Why is it so important to be faithful in attending church, Sunday School and prayer meeting?

3. Give some thought to what ministry you can have in the church. Have you given any consideration to a full-time ministry?

4. If you have doubts or misgivings about the matter of tithing, commit yourself to the Lord to give it a fair trial for at least two months. Evaluate the blessing and your attitude as the weeks go by. Watch for miracles of God's provision as you take this step of faith.

THE DOCTRINE OF THE CHURCH

The word that forms the theological name for the doctrine of the Church comes from an interesting combination of Greek words. The word *ekklesia* means "the church." The theological term "ecclesiology" is a combination of a prefix *ek*, meaning "from or out of"; the verb, *kaleo*, meaning "to call"; and the noun *logos*, meaning "the Word" or "the teaching." Combined, the word means "out of to call the word"; or if you shake it around as you must do in translating Greek, it means "the word [teaching] about those called out of," or in a reduced version, "called out ones." *The church, then, is a body of people who have been called out of the world for the purpose of bringing glory to God's name* (Eph. 1:12–14).

The New Testament uses the word "church" in two contexts, and we must be careful when we study the text not to do injustice to the doctrine by taking the word out of context and giving it an improper interpretation. It is the identical word in both instances. We will study both of the New Testament uses.

Of nearly 120 times the word "church" appears, it is used approximately 95 times referring to the *local church*. The other times it is used, it refers to the *universal church*. We shall approach them in inverse order.

The Universal Church

Definition

The first use of the word *ekklesia* we will call "universal," although we shall use it and promptly abandon it! The word has implications that are frequently misunderstood or misinterpreted. The Roman Catholics refer to themselves as the universal church, with the connotation of being the *only* church. The word "universal" means "all-inclusive," and with the common "brotherhood-of-man" interpretation, tends to make one think of the ecumenical church.

We far prefer the Biblical terminology *the Body of Christ* (1 Cor. 12:12, 13, 27). Some use other equally acceptable terms; i.e., *the mystical body* (which is still not properly descriptive because living saints are far from mystical!) or *the Bride of Christ* or *the invisible church*.

Revelation of the Body

The Body of Christ was a mystery, unknown to Biblical writers until Paul revealed it by inspiration in Ephesians. God did not reveal to Daniel or to other Old Testament prophets that He had a distinct plan to sidetrack Israel because of their spiritual infidelity and to lay aside the ultimate fulfillment of the Abrahamic covenant for a period of time until He had called out of the Gentiles a people for His name—the Church (Acts 15:14). After these "called-out ones" are raptured (1 Thess. 4:16, 17), He will restore Israel to prominence, return to reign over the earth and bring about the promised Kingdom blessings.

Composition of the Body

These Gentiles (and Jews willing to accept the Messiah Christ as their Redeemer, 2 Cor. 3:14–16) are now being formulated into the *Body of Christ*. The Body of Christ is a composite of all born-again believers from the time of the coming of the Holy Spirit at Pentecost until the Rapture. Representing a period of nearly 2,000 years, this Church has never held a worship service, observed the ordinances, sent out a missionary, had an evangelistic meeting, called a pastor, taken an offering, built a building or disciplined a member!

For that matter, the greater part of them are dead and waiting for the Rapture when, for the first time, the Body will be gathered together. They will then be translated, transformed and perfected as the Bride of Christ.

It is important to understand what it means to be a part of the Body of Christ. The term "belonging to a local church" has a certain tangibility because our physical senses are involved. We hear the music, see the preacher, touch the pew and smell the flowers. Furthermore, there have been emotional moments—we met the deacons, were voted into the church, were baptized, stood before the congregation and received the right hand of fellowship. The senses bear witness that we met certain qualifications and now enjoy certain privileges as constituent members of a local congregation.

The relationship we bear to the Body of Christ has a mysterious character because we understand it all by faith—the physical senses have nothing to do with it. The Spirit teaches us that we must be *born again* (John 3:7) and that by the Spirit we are *baptized* into the Body (1 Cor. 12:13). This birth and baptism are chronologically synonymous. Unconsciously all the soteriological events of regeneration, justification and sanctification transpired, and the Holy Spirit permanently inducted us into the family of God (the Body of Christ) by the baptism of the Holy Spirit. Spirit baptism is often misconstrued to be speaking in tongues or a "second blessing," but no such super-signs are said to accompany such baptism. Rather, those who look for them are generally those discontented to rest in the simple statements of the Word of God and are seeking some emotion-producing reaction to verify their weak faith.

The baptism of the Holy Spirit is simply that graciously wonderful act of God by which He brings us, not on account of our faith or works, into the blessed family relationship. It is *His* work, done by *His* Spirit, in the preparation of *His* bride. It is our responsibility to accept that fact and rest in it.

Anticipation of the Body

The great anticipation of every child of God is the soon return of the Savior to take us to His home in Heaven. We believe that event could happen at any moment! It is a life-changing anticipation for "he that hath this hope . . . purifies himself even as he is pure."

How little we know or anticipate, how finite is our comprehension of the transformation and the change that awaits us in that transitional moment, in that twinkling of an eye, when the trump of God calls us into His presence (1 John 3:2; Phil. 3:21; 2 Cor. 3:18). What transcendent joy to be chosen of God, to be part of the Body, His Bride, and to dwell with Him forever.

On our part and for our senses and our obedience and our service, we have the local church. This wonderful institution will become the focus of our attention in the following study.

Questions for Study

1. Did the saints of the Old Testament understand the

concept of the Church, the Body of Christ?

2. What New Testament writer was used of the Holy Spirit to reveal the Church in the Scriptures? In what book?

3. We should be familiar with other terms that describe the universal Church. Name them.

4. Can an unbeliever ever be a part of the Body of Christ?

5. How does a person become a part of the Body of Christ?

THE LOCAL CHURCH

We shift our attention now from the wider reference of the word "church" as the Body of Christ, to a more localized aspect—the local churches that exist on nearly every corner and under many different denominational names.

In order to be Biblical local churches, they must be composed of "called-out ones" or saved people. In reality many churches are not churches in the strict sense of the word *ekklesia*, for they are not composed of truly born again or "called out ones."

If the Scriptural requirements for a local church are not found in local churches, those churches are not true New Testament churches even though they may use the name! Some groups recognize this fact and now call themselves "societies," and so on. Such groups constitute a mission field, particularly if they reject such basic truths as the deity of Christ, the inspiration of the Scriptures, the Virgin Birth, the blood atonement and the personal second coming of Christ.

Characteristics of the Local Church

Definition

"A local New Testament church is a body of believers

immersed upon a credible confession of faith in Jesus Christ, having two officers (pastor and deacons), sovereign in polity, and banded together for work, worship, the observance of the ordinances and the worldwide proclamation of the gospel" (Paul R. Jackson, *The Doctrine and Administration of the Church* [Schaumburg, IL: Regular Baptist Press], p. 27).

The above definition is brief and concise but forms the heart of New Testament teaching as to what composes a true, Scripturally constituted local Baptist church. You cannot omit part of it and still have a true New Testament Baptist church. It would be good for every member of our churches to commit this definition to memory.

Relationship to the Body of Christ

The local church is to be an *organization* (brought into existence on the basis of the above definition) that has the solemn task of giving forth Christ's gospel and glorifying His name. It is important that, through its purity, life, action and dealings with the world, men see in the local church what they cannot see of the mystical body—the transformed lives of sanctified saints.

The world cannot see the Body of Christ. It is embryonic—not yet complete, invisible—as far as its structure is concerned. It would be an *organism* as compared to the organized structure of the local church. Therefore, it should be our objective to maintain and operate our local churches in such a manner that the world may see the transforming power of the gospel working literally and practically in us.

It is possible for a person to be a member of the Body of Christ and not be a member of a local church although we believe such a person is disobedient to the will and plan of

God for this age and will miss much blessing.

It is impossible to become a member of the Body of Christ on the basis of one's membership in a local church. Being in a local church does not constitute an adequate basis on which one can go to Heaven.

Membership in the Local Church

Although some deny the necessity for local church membership with the argument that there is no specific Scriptural command to join a church, we believe the New Testament assumes that relationship to be so commonly understood that it does not underscore it with a command! It is taken for granted throughout the New Testament.

There are other truths in the Bible that we accept as Biblical although they are not specifically designated by name. The Bible does not use the word "trinity," but we believe it teaches a trinitarian Godhead. The Bible does not use the phrase "substitutionary atonement," but it certainly teaches it. The Bible does not set forth proofs for the existence of God but operates on the assumption of His existence.

Verses such as 1 Corinthians 5:13 and Acts 15:22 indicate that it was the assumed practice of the early believers to be baptized and to associate themselves with a body of believers.

In the case of the misconduct of the saint in the church at Corinth, it would have been impossible for the church to have disciplined the erring brother had he not been a member of the local body. Furthermore, Matthew 18:15–17 indicates that the court of final appeals in matters of discipline is the church, and this is obviously the local church since it would be impossible to call the Body of Christ together to discipline a local believer! Thus the

Scriptures leave no doubt as to the Lord's desires relative to the believer's relationship to the local church.

Membership Requirements in a Local Baptist Church

Salvation (Acts 2:41; Colossians 1:2)

There are several things that we believe are requirements for those who wish to become members of a local church. Churches that grow careless and receive unsaved members soon degenerate into uselessness and powerlessness. It requires spiritual people to operate a spiritual body (1 Cor. 2:14), and anything less than a careful fulfillment of this requirement will soon result in little more than a religious club.

Baptism (Acts 2:41)

The early church knew nothing of unbaptized believers. When people were saved, they immediately identified themselves with believers through the public testimony of baptism. Most churches place far too little emphasis on this practical demonstration of our faith, having created a thoughtless disobedience to this cardinal command of the Word of God. There are even some Baptist churches that no longer require baptism for membership.

As soon as salvation and your eternal security are clear in your mind, you should aggressively pursue the matter of baptism into a Bible-believing Baptist church.

Sound Doctrine (Acts 2:42)

The local church should be composed only of those who subscribe to sound doctrine and who believe the Bible to be the authoritative Word of God. Careful examination should be made of each candidate relative to his doctrinal convictions. A wise practice is to determine whether or not those desiring membership in our churches are really interested in being Baptists. More churches are being watered down, their direction changed and their distinctive character altered by the silent but deadly infusion of interdenominationally minded people than by almost any other single influence of which I can think.

Our church members need to know and understand the wonderful truths of the Bible that are uniquely held by people who call themselves Baptists. We are not better than anyone else, just different! And we must not lose that difference.

Good Conduct (1 Corinthians 5:1–7)

Since we are to keep our local church memberships as pure as possible, we should seek to bring into the framework of the local church those who are living in accord with the principles of godly conduct and who are not walking in known sin. The local church is to be as perfect an example (a showcase) of the Body of Christ as we can possibly make it.

Entrance procedures for many churches have become slipshod. In some Baptist churches a total stranger can come forward at the conclusion of a service and be voted into membership simply on the basis of his desire to associate with that church without any examination of his beliefs or practices.

Other churches go through a few motions of a membership class or two, but it is my conviction that our requirements for membership should be stiff enough to screen out those who are not saved and also those who are not walking spiritually.

A thorough course in doctrine and in the operation of a Baptist church should be required so we can see our convictions perpetuated for years to come. Many members have come to our churches from other denominational orientations and know little or nothing about the distinctive operations and convictions that make us unique in the ecclesiastical world.

Since the local church and the Body of Christ are both represented in the New Testament by the same word, and since the two have such a close relationship, it follows that the entry procedures into both should be similar.

The question is often asked, "How does one become a member of the Body of Christ?" Two things are required for a sinner to be given entrance into the Bride of Christ: first, salvation (John 3:3, 7); and, second, the baptism of the Holy Spirit into the Body of Christ (1 Cor. 12:12, 13).

How, then, do we bring people into the local church? Again, as in the qualifying factors for relationship to the Body of Christ, there are two steps required for local church membership: First, a confession of faith in Jesus Christ—salvation (Acts 2:41, 42); and, second, water baptism, which is the public testimony of the fact of the baptism of the Holy Spirit and our identification with Christ in His death, burial and resurrection.

Perfect parallel exists between these two because the one is the picture of the other.

We, therefore, conclude that baptism is not only necessary for local church membership, but also that membership is mandatory at the time of baptism. This fact is not often considered to be important and is even frequently resisted by some. Careful reflection on the relationship of water baptism as a local church ordinance, however, causes us to conclude that it would be improper to baptize believers without bringing them into the relationship of a local church.

Think about these questions: Can a person be baptized by the Holy Spirit (1 Cor. 12:12, 13) without becoming a part of the *ekklesia*, the Body of Christ? Can a person be immersed by an ordinance of the local *ekklesia* without becoming a part of it? The answer should be clear!

Baptism and the Lord's Supper: Church Ordinances

These two ordinances or commands, baptism and the Lord's Supper, are not sacraments; that is, things that produce merit in our lives. But they are designed as remembrances, memorials and testimonies. They are the only ordinances given to the church for this age.

An ordinance is a ceremony established by proper authority. It is wrong to call an ordinance a sacrament. Romanists and others use the term "sacrament" to infer that special grace, merit and divine life are conferred upon those who observe certain traditional church rites.

Nowhere does the Bible promise life or grace as the result of observing these ordinances; it simply commands them to be observed. No light suggestions, these! *Commands*— 1 Corinthians 11:24, "This do . . ."; Matthew 28:19, "Go . . . teach . . . baptizing. . . ."

Baptism

The word "baptize" is the Greek word *baptizo* transliterated into English, which means "to dip," "to plunge," "to submerge." With few exceptions, scholars—

even of other denominations—agree on the meaning of the Word.

The Lord was immersed as a solid example of what He desired for His believers. The early church, without exception, practiced immersion for the first two hundred years until sinful and disobedient corruptions entered in. The deadly doctrine that baptism is necessary for salvation became the wedge that brought in unscriptural methods such as pouring and sprinkling. Today most religious people tend to equate baptism and salvation. This is serious doctrinal error and should be studiously avoided.

Baptism is a symbol or picture of our relationship with Jesus Christ in His death, burial and resurrection. The actual burial in the baptismal waters is a graphic description of this fact. Baptism further serves as a public testimony of our faith in Him and our desire to be identified with Him.

We believe that baptism is important for believer obedience and that to disregard it, call it insignificant or suggest that it is anything less than mandatory is to say that the commands of the Lord are only relatively important.

Why don't we baptize babies? This question is often asked. The Bible is crystal clear: "Believe, and be baptized." The command indicates that those too young to place their faith in Christ are not candidates for baptism. There must first be a knowledgeable faith in Jesus Christ.

In most instances this desire for baby baptism stems out of the problem already mentioned relative to salvation by works. The parents fail to realize that a few drops of water cannot save a baby. Instead, God's grace covers the little one until he is old enough to know of his need of a Savior.

This is also why many churches do not have baby dedications. The uninstructed visitor, the ungrounded believer, impressionable children, the sometimes-carnal young parents, the mixed marriages, the emphasis on the dedication of the baby instead of the dedication of the parents, the frilly little confirmation-type dresses—these and other reasons caused me to get out of the baby dedication business years ago!

If a Christian mother and father want to make a spiritual decision to yield their lives into God's hands to faithfully and earnestly train and lead their child into a knowledge of Jesus Christ, let them come forward—with their baby if they desire—at the closing invitation and make this decision before God's people. This action I heartily recommend.

The Lord's Supper

As baptism is a symbol of our *union* with Christ, so the Lord's Supper is a symbol of our *communion* with Him.

It is a memorial feast commemorating the body of the Lord and the shed blood of our Savior. It clearly and vividly brings the matters and the cost of our redemption into view. It is obviously a table for believers only and is to be kept in force until Christ returns.

A careless attitude toward the Lord's Table will result in sickness or possibly even death. It is a serious thing to treat the Lord's Supper casually. Read 1 Corinthians 11:29–34.

Before coming to the Lord's Table we should have a time of self-inspection (examination) and confession (cleansing) that allows us to approach our fellowship with Christ with clean hands and a pure heart.

Local churches have varying practices regarding the

time the Lord's Table is scheduled into the worship program. One of the worst practices is the one most frequently used. After a full service of hymns, special music, announcements and a lengthy message (often on a subject not even remotely related to the death of Christ, and after the worship hour is long spent and roasts are already approaching burnt-offering status), only then, are the deacons invited to the platform to serve Communion.

When little spiritual preparation and time are given to it, the beautiful service of the Lord's Table becomes a burdensome appendage on the worship service, which people are eager to have concluded.

The Lord's Table ought to be the central part of the service, and sufficient time should be given to make it meaningful to every believer. We are told that by observing the Lord's Table "we do preach the Lord's death." If so, let the Lord's Table preach and become the service, not just a squeezed-in afterthought.

Conclusion

These two ordinances are the domain of the local church. Other groups—Bible conferences, gatherings of ministers, schools, individuals and the like—are not granted the prerogative of these divine institutions. True believers should refrain from participation in an unscriptural practice of even a Scriptural ordinance.

It is not Scripturally proper for someone to baptize another person in a swimming pool or anywhere else, without proper examination and the authority of a local church. Anyone in a local church may do the actual baptizing as long as the church has given approval of the candidate.

It is not proper for a pastor to take communion to members sick at home or in the hospital, for it is a local church ordinance.

Questions for Study

1. Can anyone become a member of a local church?

2. Name the ordinances of a Baptist church.

3. Why are ordinances not called sacraments?

4. Baptism is a symbol. What does it picture?

5. What does the grape juice represent in the communion service?

Chapter 7

THE POLITY OF THE LOCAL CHURCH

As we continue our study of the local church, we now touch upon some of the practical elements of its life. These things are as important to the continuity, perpetuity and purity of the church as the matters of membership that we have already discussed.

Forms of Local Church Government

There are four basic forms of church government, one of which will categorize almost any church group:

Government Form	Authority Rests In
Papal	One dictatorial voice; e.g., the pope
Episcopalian	Ruling bishops
Presbyterian	Synods, presbyteries, classes
Congregational	The local congregation

As you move up the list from congregational to papal government, you will note that absolute power over the church is concentrated in fewer people until finally it rests in one man.

Obviously our convictions lead us to believe in and practice congregational government. We recognize the role of church officers and their importance in a smoothly functioning organization, but the final voice of authority in the local church rests with the congregation.

There is a beautiful system of checks and balances written into the Word and into local church life. While the church congregation has final authority, it recognizes the Scriptural role of the pastor and remembers the injunction "Obey them that have the rule over you" (Heb. 13:17).

This is the operational procedure: moral and spiritual authority rests in the pastor until such time as the church feels he has overstepped in either doctrine or polity. They then have the right to step in and make decisions. If a major issue exists on which the pastor and a majority of the people differ, it might be wise for the pastor to leave before a church split develops. There are few valid reasons, if any, for which a pastor should be responsible for a church split!

A good, spiritual congregation and a good, spiritual pastor can work along happily under the God-designed program of pastoral rule and congregational authority and know real joy and harmony. It should be clearly understood that the pastor is not an employee of the church or a hired hand. He is "employed" by God, Who gives pastors to churches as spiritual "undershepherds." The pastor is responsible to God for the operation of the local church over which the Lord has placed him, and every area of its life should be accountable to the pastor (Heb. 13:17).

Increasing numbers of pastors have the mistaken impression that they are the final authority in the church. They make all the decisions, relegate the God-designed office of deacon to an inconspicuous role, bulldoze church members and sometimes even write the church checks. In a few cases, the pastor even has the church property in his name.

The reverse problem has also become serious in many Baptist churches when they become controlled by boards. The New Testament knows nothing about a board of deacons.

General Motors is run by a board, but a local church—never! The best thing that could happen would be to remove the term "board" from the church vocabulary as it relates to deacons and trustees.

Deacons, as the Greek word implies, are servants of the church. Who ever heard of a board of servants?

When godly deacons recognize the Scriptural role of the pastor as a God-given authority in the church, pray for him, cooperate with him, encourage him and counsel with him, we will have returned to a baptistic form of government where the church makes the decisions under the leadership of God's man. The Lord intended that His sheep be led by a shepherd, not by a committee or board!

When the boards are the power and make policy decisions affecting the church, we have drifted one step into presbyterian or synodical government and closer to elder rule, which is unscriptural.

Officers of the Church

The New Testament requires a local church have a minimum of two offices: pastor and deacons (Phil. 1:1).

First Timothy 3:1–13 details the requirements for these offices. However, additional officers are not unscriptural. The law requires trustees for a corporation; a clerk is necessary for good records; a treasurer simplifies the handling of funds, and so on; but Scripture mandates pastors and deacons in the formation and operation of a true local Baptist church.

The great diversity of offices in various denominations is a result of failure to adhere to the Word and an expedient attitude that the end justifies the means. Much of the problem revolves around terms. The confusion is greatly simplified when you understand that the Biblical words "pastor," "elder" and "bishop" refer to the same officer. It is one man but three different roles.

In 1 Peter 5:1–4, while referring to *pastors*, the Spirit also calls them *elders*, and in verse 2 the word "oversight" is *episkopeo*, which is translated *bishop* elsewhere in the Bible. Titus 1:5–7 speaks of elders and bishops in the same reference. See also Acts 20:17–28. *Elder* indicates the dignity of the office; *bishop*, the duties (oversight); and *pastor*, the relationship to the flock. All three terms refer to the person we most commonly call "pastor." When you meet me on the street, please don't call out to me in stentorian tones, "Hello there, Bishop Elder Pastor Mark Jackson," for I would probably run. But at least you would be correct!

Financing the Local Church

Accuracy and businesslike methods in handling the Lord's money are requirements for sound fiscal operation. Not only do they honor the Lord (1 Cor. 14:40), but they also will likely increase the income of the church as donors have confidence in the competence of the officers.

A budget should be adopted each year by church vote. The congregation should agree to trust the Lord to meet this budget and then systematically bring their tithes and offerings, giving them to the Lord through the church. We do not tithe or give to "meet a budget" but to be obedient stewards!

No fund-raising pledge systems, rummage sales, or pancake dinners should be held to help meet the budget. The giving of tithes is the God-designed way of meeting the needs of a local church. The budget is simply a guide to give some indication of the anticipated annual expense and is not "the law of the Medes and the Persians."

Churches handle their finances in different ways. Some have only one fund that all tithes and offerings go through. All local expenses and missions commitments are paid out of the same fund. Other churches have several funds: general, missions, building, etc. The problem with this latter system is that some give all their money to missions and nothing to general, or all to the building and nothing to missions. Some feel it is more spiritual to support missions than a building! Some people become angry with the pastor and do not want "their money" to go to his support, so they give everything to the building fund! The first system resolves these problems.

A system of envelopes is used in most churches and is for your convenience and protection. The financial secretary records your gifts and at the end of the year provides a record of giving for your income tax report. These records are to be used for no other purpose and should not be made available to the public in any way.

The tithe—and beyond that, offerings—is a Scriptural basis of one's giving. Malachi 3:10 and 1 Corinthians 16:1 and 2 clearly establish the Biblical precedent of a systematic first-day-of-the-week giving program.

Questions for Study

1. Name two churches or groups who practice papal government.

2. What form of church government is common to true Baptist churches?

3. Who is the final authority in a local New Testament church?

4. Why should the men we select as deacons not be called a board?

5. Name the three terms the New Testament uses to describe our pastor.

6. In planning our giving to the Lord, what should the basic gift be?

7. Do you tithe to your local church?

Chapter 8

ASSOCIATIONAL RELATIONSHIPS

Time will increasingly reveal that one of the curses of our age in the realm of the local church is interdenominationalism. Going by different names, undenominational or nondenominational, it is the same breed and should be understood by soundly structured churches to be exactly what it is—dangerous! Under the syrupy guise of a cooperative venture and the removal of an assumed stigma of denominational relationships, the unthinking and gullible are led down the primrose path to compromise and the loss of some important and basic foundational convictions.

We stand categorically opposed to the ecumenical, one-world-church idea of the liberal theological establishment as embodied in the National Council of Churches and the World Council of Churches. We also shun the compromise position of such groups as the National Association of Evangelicals, who feel that our position of "separation" is too antagonistic and outmoded and should be replaced by their objective of "infiltration," a process whereby they aim to infiltrate the apostasy with truth(!?). This procedure is not only untenable and impracticable but unscriptural, for the Word clearly commands us to be separate from worldliness, unbelief and compromise.

The Problems of Interdenominational Groups and Councils

Interdenominationalism is merely ecumenicalism being spawned within the framework of redemptive truth. The basic framework of truth is there, but so are the subtleties, the danger of minimizing truths and distinctives and the breakdown of local church sovereignty. These and other areas cause growing concern as we witness the multiplicity of interdenominational and para-church programs that proliferate at an alarming rate, largely because they are so theologically broadminded that they attract a wide variety of attention and response.

In each period of time the believing church has been faced with a new problem of this variety. In our day, groups like Campus Crusade, while attempting good goals, have created confusion with their programs of evangelism, which even include unbelievers. The mixing of belief and unbelief has never been God's program in evangelism and will not work. Inter-Varsity, with its strong anti-local church attitude, cannot be accepted as an ally. Billy Graham-type crusades, while used of God in the salvation of many people (and contrary to popular notion, we praise the Lord when sinners are converted, no matter how a sovereign Lord brings it about), cannot be approved as something with which we would cooperate because of the unbiblical practices of sending converts back to unbelieving churches, Graham's unbiblical fraternization with the apostate ecumenical church and his soft attitude and statements about the Roman Catholic Church.

Many such organizations that operate entirely outside the realm of the local church have been widely accepted by the churches—even our own churches. However, we are not at liberty to do wrong even if seeming good may come out of it.

In saying this we may have mentioned some of your "favorites." However, I believe future history will bear out that some of the most destructive influences on the Christian scene will have been perpetrated by organizations that have set themselves up outside the framework of the local church or who have sought to supersede or bypass the local church and failed to obey the Scriptural mandate of separation from the apostasy. No matter how worthy they may seem or how much good they purportedly accomplish, be sure that the ministries you support bear absolute and total fidelity to the Word of God and His program for this age—the local church.

Often the sop is offered that these "inter-, un- and non-" programs "win souls," and thereby people excuse the slipshod manner in which they are run, the doctrinal twists one must stomach or the compromises one must make in order to fellowship with them. We do not believe the Lord is pleased. *He expects obedience, and you do not have to compromise to be obedient. Furthermore, within the framework of total obedience, God will give you souls for your labor* (see 1 Sam. 15:22).

Over the years we have become increasingly convinced of the Scripturality of this position, and while it is not popular in many quarters, we are convinced it is Biblical. The pressures to "give in" come from every angle: outside and inside. But the cost is too great, and the cause of Christ too precious to compromise.

It should be said that these convictions are not the result of the association of our churches with the General Association of Regular Baptist Churches. These are Biblical convictions, and we would hold them even if there were no GARBC. The Association is merely a fellowship of churches who believe the same thing and agree to seek spiritual fellowship together.

We believe that local churches should be independent and autonomous in character; that they are under the guidance of their Head, Jesus Christ; that they are under the visible leadership of godly pastors. We also believe individual, independent Baptist churches may commit themselves to a voluntary fellowship with other churches of like faith and order in what we commonly call an association—although the word "fellowship" more fittingly describes the resulting relationship.

This seems to be characteristic of the way the early churches in the book of Acts worked together. There were no bishops governing the pastors or churches, but fellowship was based on a unity of faith in Christ (see Acts 15).

How the Divisions Came About

Through the years many divisions over doctrinal issues or personalities have resulted in a denominationally divided ecclesiastical world. Satan has surely had his sticky fingers in this and has caused untold confusion and hurt to the cause of Christ.

In the early 1900s, the modernists and the fundamentalists were engaged in theological battles. It was simple. You either believed the Bible to be the Word of God, or you did not; either Christ was God, or He was not. You were in one camp or the other. The Devil knew that was too easy, so he further complicated things by dividing both groups.

The *modernists* developed an offshoot called, among other names, *neoorthodoxy;* on the other hand, the *fundamentalists* saw a new group arise called the *neoevangelicals.* The *neoorthodox*—with little or no doctrinal convictions and in too many cases very little scruples (e.g., "situation ethics"; actual encouragement of premarital and extramarital sex; involvement in civil disobedience; encouragement of minorities to revolt using force, if necessary; jazz worship services; total fellowship across all doctrinal and denominational lines, including Muhammadanism, Catholicism, Judaism, etc.), and the *neoevangelicals*—who have fundamental orthodoxy and Bible truth but no convictions about separation from unbelief and who find one of their greatest delights in "dialoguing" with the neoorthodox and liberal, while poking fun at their former associates in the fundamentalist ranks—*see themselves as bridges for cooperation and, possibly, ultimate amalgamation.*

MODERNISTS	NEO-ORTHODOX	NEO-EVANGELICALISM	FUNDAMENTALISTS
Bible is **not** Word of God	Bible **contains** Word of God	Bible inspiration should be **reexamined**	Bible **is** the Word of God

We must not place ourselves in this hodgepodge. We need not, yea rather, *we must not*. The Lord has given us a specific command to a specific task: *Make* disciples, *baptize, teach* (Matt. 28:19, 20). To seek to fulfill that command in *any* kind of relationship with those who feel that salvation and regeneration are to be found through social change or good works *is impossible*.

The Particular Problem of Neoevangelicalism

Neoevangelicalism has only recently developed in fundamental circles. The thrust of neoevangelicals is distinctly different from our fundamental position of separation in that they openly befriend the ecumenist and openly criticize the fundamentalist. The movement is growing rapidly because it accepts such a wide variety of theological positions within its ranks.

Dr. Reginald Matthews, former assistant to the national representative of the GARBC and former professor at Baptist Bible Seminary in Pennsylvania, said of the difficulty of technically identifying this group, "Neoevangelicalism cannot be detected by what they [neoevangelicals] declare or deny, but rather by the fact that they will cooperate with anybody no matter what they declare or deny."

In order to bring these things into focus, on page 72 is a chart that gives the recent history of Baptist churches. It can hardly be exhaustive, for there are more than forty bodies of Baptists in America alone, including such small groups as the Two-Seed-in-the-Spirit Predestinarian Baptist Churches!

One of the things that proved to be so dangerous in the early days of the Northern Baptist Convention, now the American Baptist Churches, was the denominational control of its schools and mission agencies. The power of a few men, invariably modernists, over the multimillion dollar missions/schools operation was disastrous. The schools succumbed to a liberal philosophy and the mission agencies sent out the product. "Inclusivism," a major factor in the determination of early separatists to abandon the apostate camp, was the practice of "including" on missionary status any and all, no matter what they believed. Even Communists were supported on the field as missionaries!

After struggling with the controlling modernists for a number of years, twenty-two churches withdrew from the Northern Baptist Convention and in 1932 formed a new fellowship, the *General Association of Regular Baptist Churches*. Recognizing the inherent problems in the Convention, the founders of the new fellowship determined from its inception to be *only* a fellowship of churches and to stay entirely out of the operation of schools and mission agencies. Therefore, it handles *no funds* for the churches, has *no mission agencies* and operates *no schools*. We recognize and encourage the support of existing Baptist schools and mission agencies that hold the same pattern of truth as the churches, but we do so without any hierarchical control whatsoever.

Certain schools and mission boards are examined and approved each year as being worthy of consideration and support and as being qualified institutions to which we can safely send our youth. Each local church is responsible to do as it wishes in the matter of the support of the various institutions without the dictates of a convention.

Another Convention problem was the state and local conventions that helped maintain the overall power of the deeply entrenched liberalism. In seeking to stand clearly upon the platform of the sovereignty of the local church, the GARBC has no state or local associations. Any regional groups, such as the Iowa Association of Regular Baptist Churches or the Michigan Association of Regular Baptist Churches, are similar in name only and have absolutely no organizational connection with the national Association although they are entirely in agreement with it.

Another group, the Conservative Baptist Association, determined from their beginning in 1947 that they would not require their churches to withdraw from the liberal Convention of which they were also a part. They sought to continue the effort to clean up the Convention from within. Neither did they learn the folly of the missions and schools problem, but promptly set up their own Conservative Baptist mission societies and Conservative Baptist schools, which have caused them grief from the outset and which are part of the reason for their multi-divisions today.

As of now, most of the CBA churches have seen the hopeless nature of their intent to clean up the ABC from within and have withdrawn from it.

For those of us within the fellowship of the General Association of Regular Baptist Churches, there is a happy relationship based upon mutual loyalty to the Lord Jesus Christ and His Word. As long as such a spirit continues in the Association, we will be happy to stay in the Fellowship. If it should drift away from its loyalty to the Word, its position on separation or its determination to maintain the absolute independence and sovereignty of its churches, many of us would leave.

Questions for Study

1. What does "ecumenical" mean?

2. Does the General Association of Regular Baptist Churches operate any colleges?

3. What is the neoorthodox view of the Bible?

4. What is the fundamentalist's view of the Scriptures?

Chapter 9

THE GARBC AND OTHER CHURCH BODIES

Before continuing our examination of the ecclesiastical situation and the relationship of various church groups, let me add a few more background remarks about the GARBC.

The Beginnings of the GARBC

The General Association of Regular Baptist Churches (see chart on p. 72) was begun in 1932 with twenty-two churches. It has grown now to almost sixteen hundred churches, each one of which stands uncompromisingly for the Word as the inspired and infallible revelation from God.

It was begun as a separation movement, born out of necessity when the Northern Baptist Convention insisted on its liberal course. Obeying the Scriptures, these churches set up a fellowship on a strong separatist, Biblical statement of faith, and God has blessed their step of obedience (2 Cor. 6:14—7:1).

Because of its stubborn insistence on separation from apostasy and its strong determination that the "Word alone" is its guide, the GARBC is often criticized and ridiculed. The associating churches have been described as "fighters." The word is sadly misused and twisted out of context, for they are not fighters unless you believe that a strong defense of the faith is

RECENT HISTORY OF BAPTIST CHURCHES

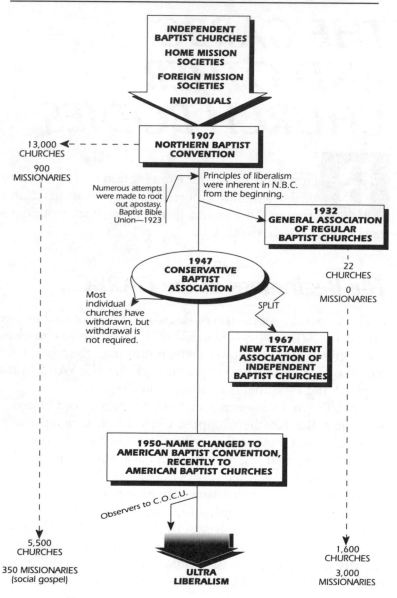

INDEPENDENT BAPTIST CHURCHES

HOME MISSION SOCIETIES

FOREIGN MISSION SOCIETIES

INDIVIDUALS

1907 NORTHERN BAPTIST CONVENTION

13,000 CHURCHES

900 MISSIONARIES

Numerous attempts were made to root out apostasy. Baptist Bible Union—1923

Principles of liberalism were inherent in N.B.C. from the beginning.

1932 GENERAL ASSOCIATION OF REGULAR BAPTIST CHURCHES

22 CHURCHES

0 MISSIONARIES

1947 CONSERVATIVE BAPTIST ASSOCIATION

Most individual churches have withdrawn, but withdrawal is not required.

SPLIT

1967 NEW TESTAMENT ASSOCIATION OF INDEPENDENT BAPTIST CHURCHES

1950–NAME CHANGED TO AMERICAN BAPTIST CONVENTION, RECENTLY TO AMERICAN BAPTIST CHURCHES

Observers to C.O.C.U.

5,500 CHURCHES

350 MISSIONARIES (social gospel)

ULTRA LIBERALISM

1,600 CHURCHES

3,000 MISSIONARIES

"fighting." Those who use the term to describe us usually do not know anything about us from firsthand knowledge and are the sort who are generally careless about facts. A sound constitution preserves the continuity of the Fellowship, and a clear doctrinal statement maintains its doctrinal position. A wonderful Fellowship is possible because of the unity of faith that binds us together.

In recent years a few churches have withdrawn from the Association, and some other pastors have threatened to lead their churches out of the GARBC over soteriological matters. Some feel we are too Calvinistic; others, that we are too Arminian! Several national periodicals rushed into print with headlines that the Association had split over Calvinism, which was, of course, not true. There are divisions of opinion, but that is hardly a split! There have always been some differences of opinion over some of those doctrinal issues, but that latitude has always existed.

Historically, the GARBC has been characterized by what was commonly called and commonly understood as "moderate Calvinism." Most of our churches hold to the majority of the typical Calvinistic outline of doctrines while rejecting "limited atonement."

It is my conviction that the GARBC is still possessed of a strong Calvinistic position and that the overwhelming majority of our pastors and churches are still classed as "moderate Calvinists," call them what you will!

In even more recent times there has been a group of pastors who have felt strongly that the Association is in a "drifting" mode as it relates to separation. It is probably true that some men and churches do not hold that doctrine as clearly as all our churches formerly did.

There are several reasons this is true. A new generation of men has arisen. They have never faced much of a battle with liberalism and have not "smelled the smoke" of those problems. Churches call pastors who have not been indoctrinated in this important doctrine. Some feel the battles with such issues are past and are unimportant. Softened convictions on the part of many of our church members reflect the failure of our pulpits to teach adequately. All these reasons indicate that we need to concentrate on these matters and to mend some fences.

The GARBC has weathered other divisive storms in the past, lost a church or two, closed ranks and gone on. It is my conviction that it will do so again.

The Organization of the GARBC

It is necessary to understand the organization of our Association in order to appreciate it. The framers of the constitution were determined to maintain the autonomy and sovereignty of the local churches. Therefore, no man, council or group of churches can make any decision that is binding upon the churches. There are no state secretaries or officials to give orders. There is no bishop placing pastors. There is no centralized budget to which funds are sent.

Its Annual Meeting

The Association is loosely knit together for fellowship and meets only once a year for a week-long Bible and missions conference. When it is over, the church members go back to their local churches, labor with their pastors and do their jobs in the local church. We are careful not to compromise these convictions in any way. We are sovereign, independent local churches, but we enjoy the fellowship of sixteen hundred other churches of "like faith and practice."

The annual conference is becoming increasingly popular with the church members and is designed with them in mind. It is not just a week of theology for the pastors, but a wonderful time of fellowship. Plan to attend if you can. It meets the last week of June in various parts of the country.

In recent years it has been held in Seattle, Washington; Springfield, Illinois; Grand Rapids, Michigan; Ames, Iowa; Anaheim, California; and Columbus, Ohio.

National Representative

The only paid offices in the Association are a national representative, a secretary and, on occasion, an assistant. The job of the national representative is to represent the Association in the various churches where he is invited and to help in areas of problems if they desire to use his services or ask for his advice. He is very careful, however, to refrain from entering into a local problem or even going *to* that church unless he is invited. He will not even recommend a pastor to a church unless he is asked for a recommendation. Thus, local church sovereignty is not infringed upon in any way whatsoever.

Council of Eighteen

The Council of Eighteen is the only elected leadership of the Association. These are men elected by the churches to serve a two-year term (after two terms they automatically rotate and cannot be reelected for at least one year). They are nominated by the churches and elected at the annual meeting. The Association frowns upon using politics in the election process. It also seeks the free voice of the churches and their voting messengers in the determining of God's will in their selection.

Their duties are merely those given to them by the constitution: e.g., counseling with the national representative, planning the annual meeting, investigating the approved mission agencies and schools each year, and representing the churches before government in such matters as the chaplaincy.

Thus their duties lie not so much in policy-making but in caring for the details of the operation of such a Fellowship. We can rejoice at the wisdom given to twenty-two pastors and churches in setting up a constitution and Fellowship that so meaningfully protects the rights and sovereignty of the local church but provides an area for fellowship across the country where we may move among our churches and know that we are in the midst of people who love the Lord and His Word. Furthermore, the annual checkup on mission boards and schools continues to provide a service for us, letting us know that these agencies, while maintaining no organizational connection to us, are in agreement with us in doctrinal, practical and procedural realms.

Regular Baptist Press

Regular Baptist Press was begun in 1952 to print Sunday School material for churches, but is not a part of "associational officialdom." It is a ministry set up by the churches themselves who had grown weary of getting literature from interdenominational presses that, while teaching the Bible, tended to minimize Baptist distinctives. It is interesting to note that while we have sixteen hundred churches in our Fellowship (and all of those churches do not use our Sunday School literature), almost seven thousand churches now use RBP Sunday School material—the reason being that it is true to the Word of God, while many other printing houses have drifted into compromise positions and shallow theology. RBP also prints take-home papers, Vacation Bible School materials and books. The *Baptist Bulletin*, a monthly magazine published by the Press, keeps readers informed of activities within the Fellowship and provides inspirational Bible teaching for the family.

Gospel Literature Services

In 1973 the Council of Eighteen inaugurated a free literature service for missionaries serving under approved missionary agencies. Millions of pieces of literature have been sent around the world resulting in the salvation of hundreds of souls.

Funds with which to carry on this service for our missionaries are solicited from churches and interested individuals, who are the only source of support.

It is the privilege of this writer to serve as the executive director of this international ministry, representing the work in the churches and raising funds to meet the literature needs for the missionaries.

Approved Schools, Missions and Service Ministries

The GARBC does not have schools or mission agencies as do many church organizations. That was one of the problems in the Convention that years ago caused the GARBC to be formed. So in establishing the Association, the leaders determined to have no such agencies as part of the organization. Instead, already existing independent Baptist schools and mission boards were found that held the same doctrinal position as the GARBC. These were "approved" and recommended to the churches as trustworthy and worthy of support. The churches, therefore, support such institutions and send their youth to them independently without the intervention of a national church body. Once again the sovereignty of the local church is upheld. These agencies are investigated annually for continued approval.

Following is a list of the presently approved schools and mission agencies. Approval does not mean that others may not be good but that these are Baptist organizations that are in total accord with our position—and we with them. They are recommended to the churches by the Council of Eighteen. In turn, we encourage young people to go to these schools and to use these mission boards.

Approved Independent Baptist Schools

1. Baptist Bible College and Seminary
   Clarks Summit, Pennsylvania
2. Cedarville College
   Cedarville, Ohio
3. Faith Baptist Bible College and Seminary
   Ankeny, Iowa
4. Grand Rapids Baptist College and Seminary
   Grand Rapids, Michigan
5. Northwest Baptist Seminary
   Tacoma, Washington
6. Spurgeon Baptist Bible College
   Mulberry, Florida
7. Western Baptist College
   Salem, Oregon

Approved Independent Baptist Mission Agencies

1. Association of Baptists for World Evangelism (ABWE)
   Cherry Hill, New Jersey
2. Baptist Mid-Missions (BMM)
   Cleveland, Ohio
3. Baptist Mission of North America (BMNA)
   Elyria, Ohio
4. Committee on Missionary Evangelism (COME)
   Grand Rapids, Michigan

5. Continental Baptist Missions (CBM)
   Comstock Park, Michigan
6. Evangelical Baptist Missions (EBM)
   Kokomo, Indiana

Recognizing a special need to care for problems within the local churches, the Council of Eighteen has recently broadened the approval procedure to include some social agencies that are also recommended to the churches. Following is a list of those presently approved:

Approved Independent Baptist Service Ministries

1. Baptist Children's Home and Family Ministries, Inc.
   Valparaiso, Indiana
2. Baptists for Life
   Grand Rapids, Michigan
3. Michigan Christian Home Association
   Grand Rapids, Michigan
4. Baptist Family Agency
   Seattle, Washington
5. Shepherds Baptist Ministries
   Union Grove, Wisconsin

INTERDENOMINATIONAL CHURCH RELATIONSHIPS

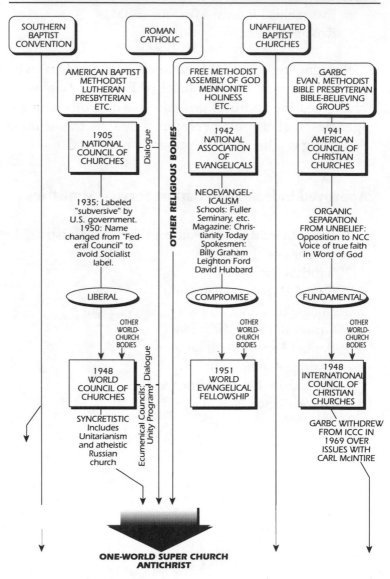

SOUTHERN BAPTIST CONVENTION

ROMAN CATHOLIC

UNAFFILIATED BAPTIST CHURCHES

AMERICAN BAPTIST
METHODIST
LUTHERAN
PRESBYTERIAN
ETC.

FREE METHODIST
ASSEMBLY OF GOD
MENNONITE
HOLINESS
ETC.

GARBC
EVAN. METHODIST
BIBLE PRESBYTERIAN
BIBLE-BELIEVING
GROUPS

1905
NATIONAL
COUNCIL OF
CHURCHES

Dialogue

OTHER RELIGIOUS BODIES

1942
NATIONAL
ASSOCIATION
OF
EVANGELICALS

1941
AMERICAN
COUNCIL OF
CHRISTIAN
CHURCHES

1935: Labeled
"subversive" by
U.S. government.
1950: Name
changed from "Fed-
eral Council" to
avoid Socialist
label.

NEOEVANGEL-
ICALISM
Schools: Fuller
Seminary, etc.
Magazine: Chris-
tianity Today
Spokesmen:
Billy Graham
Leighton Ford
David Hubbard

ORGANIC
SEPARATION
FROM UNBELIEF:
Opposition to NCC
Voice of true faith
in Word of God

LIBERAL

COMPROMISE

FUNDAMENTAL

OTHER
WORLD-
CHURCH
BODIES

OTHER
WORLD-
CHURCH
BODIES

OTHER
WORLD-
CHURCH
BODIES

1948
WORLD
COUNCIL OF
CHURCHES

Ecumenical Councils;
Unity Programs; Dialogue

1951
WORLD
EVANGELICAL
FELLOWSHIP

1948
INTERNATIONAL
COUNCIL OF
CHRISTIAN
CHURCHES

SYNCRETISTIC
Includes
Unitarianism
and atheistic
Russian
church

GARBC WITHDREW
FROM ICCC IN
1969 OVER
ISSUES WITH
CARL McINTIRE

**ONE-WORLD SUPER CHURCH
ANTICHRIST**

The GARBC and Other Religious Bodies

The chart on page 80 is brief and covers only a few basic facts about some of the complexities of today's ecclesiastical world. There are three basic divisions in Protestantism today:

National Council of Churches

The National Council of Churches and its worldwide organizational counterpart, the World Council of Churches, represent the *liberal religious element*. They basically reject the Bible as the Word of God and Christ as deity.

American Council of Christian Churches

The American Council of Christian Churches (which was formerly associated with the International Council of Christian Churches, but which parted company over some unfortunate personality problems) is a sound, Biblical organization and is *fundamental* in its position. Both are still true to the Word, and both can be classified as Bible believers standing for an inspired and infallible Bible, the deity of Jesus Christ and atonement through the blood of Christ. Many GARBC churches are affiliated with the ACCC although relationship with the ACCC is not automatic. Each GARBC church must individually decide whether or not it wishes to associate with the ACCC—one further acknowledgement of the totally independent character of the local churches.

National Association of Evangelicals

The middle-of-the-road groups, the National Association of Evangelicals and the World Evangelical Fellowship, are non-separatists whose stated objective is to "infiltrate" the liberal groups with the gospel. We are to remember that the Bible teaches separation *from* unbelief, not infiltration *of* it! They are friendly to the liberal and critical of the fundamentalist.

Questions for Study

1. In what year was the GARBC organized? How many churches were involved at its origination?

2. What one word describes the position of the GARBC as opposed to other church bodies?

3. What is the name of the present national representative?

4. Does the GARBC have a centralized budget to which the local churches send funds?

5. How many of the approved schools can you name without looking?

6. How many approved mission agencies can you name?

7. What do the following letters stand for?
   NCC_____
   NAE_____
   ACCC_____
   GARBC_____

Chapter 10

BAPTIST DISTINCTIVES

Many Christians are guilty of taking the path of least resistance in the matter of their church relationship. Because of family ties, sentimental relationships or other attachments, they remain in churches that have drifted away from the truth. In other cases, members of a sound church can give no "reason for the hope that lieth in them," and do not know what they believe or have any solid Scripture-based convictions. Many are there just because that is where they were raised.

May the Lord give us Spirit-born convictions as to what we believe and some divine grit to hold them against both the open attack of the enemy and the soft attack of rationalization from within. Doctrinal softness and a gutless "accommodationalism" are the sins of our day. We need to know what we believe and how to defend those beliefs using the Word of God.

There is a certain group of doctrines that we call Baptist distinctives. These have historically been believed by Baptists. Over the centuries those who believed these doctrines found their spiritual "home" in the ranks of the Baptists. Those who have disagreed with even one point have eventually caused some form of division or finally left. Like the little sections of an orange, these doctrines go together to make up a whole.

Other church groups may believe nearly all of these, but a difference of opinion in even one area has generally been sufficient to drop them into some other denominational niche.

Perhaps it should be said here that we do not believe that there are going to be only Baptists in Heaven or that we have a corner on truth. Denominational "tags" are semantic conveniences describing the various theological persuasions. Men are saved through faith in Jesus Christ and His cleansing blood. Baptists who *do not* believe this will go to Hell, and Presbyterians who *do* will go to Heaven!

The name "Baptist" is a word describing a great heritage. Many of our forefathers died bloody deaths because they held these truths to be precious. Although many Baptists have abandoned these historic truths, *we have not.* We stand in direct descent of those stalwarts of the faith of generations past.

Sometimes those who are not in accord with the total embodiment of the doctrinal stand linked with the name "Baptist" chafe at some of these doctrines or even the use of the name "Baptist." We believe that in these days of confusion, a clear, definitive name declares who we are, what we believe and where we stand. It is much like the various labels on the cans in the grocery store that declare content, quality and brand name. Without such labels, shopping would be a catastrophe.

Let us remember that in holding our particular system of convictions, we should be careful to give no needless offense or show antagonism toward others who do not agree with us. Proper spiritual balance will let us hold strong doctrines but yet be gracious to those not in our camp.

Following is a brief examination of the various truths that are described as Baptist distinctives.

The Inspiration, Accuracy and Authority of the Bible

While any church that names the name of Christ should declare inspiration of the Bible to be a tenet of its faith, the

Baptists give unique emphasis to this doctrine. No group that denies the inspiration of the Scriptures should even be called Christian.

Two words basically describe our convictions about inspiration:

Verbal

Meaning the Holy Spirit controlled the writers to the extent that the very words were given by God. Though He used the style and language of each man so controlled, the very mind of God was inerrantly put on paper for us.

Plenary

Meaning all or total, i.e., the entire Bible is *fully* and *equally* inspired. Read the following references: Matthew 5:18; John 10:35; 2 Timothy 3:16; 2 Peter 1:21.

The centrality of the Word and its authority in church and life even affects the architectural design of church buildings. Churches in many other denominations have two pulpits—each set to one side of the platform with the focus of attention placed on an altar, cross, crucifix or candles in the center. It is a satanic subtlety that detracts from the importance of the preaching of the Word and emphasizes a priestly function rather than the "foolishness of preaching." It is for this reason that we resist the use of altars, crosses, candles and pictures of Christ and keep the pulpit in the center.

We must resolutely resist this subtle satanic attack against the absolute centrality and authority of the Word of God.

The Sovereignty of God

Briefly stated, an intelligent, personal, rational, all-powerful God has a divine plan for man and the universe, and

He has the power, the authority and the will to fulfill it.

God's sovereignty deals with many truths and, of course, the entire universe. However, sovereignty, as it relates to the salvation of man, is the most volatile part of this wonderful truth.

Many have fallen prey to an interpretation of the free will of man as it relates to his salvation, as though God left the outcome of His plans to save men to the choice of the unregenerate, finite, fickle heart of man.

It is *God* Who provides salvation; it is *God* Who has chosen us to salvation; it is *God* Who, through the Spirit, brings conviction upon us; it is *God* Who seeks us, not we who seek God; it is *God* Who keeps us saved "by the power of God" (John 10:27–30; Rom. 3:11; Eph. 1:4; Phil. 1:6; Heb. 7:25; 1 Pet. 1:5).

It is strange that otherwise clear thinking believers are afraid to exercise simple faith when it comes to sovereignty. If God is GOD, then He is sovereign, or He is not God after all. Furthermore, He is sovereign in wisdom, power and grace. "Shall not the Judge of all the earth do right?" (Gen. 18:25).

Learn to rest in the perfect peace of Ephesians 1:11: He "worketh all things after the counsel of his own will."

A Pure, Regenerate, Baptized Church Membership

A church is a spiritual organization, not a club or a social group. It is necessary, therefore, to maintain certain spiritual standards for membership.

The Scriptures detail what those standards are. Examine the practice of the early church, and you will see that invariably it was those who were saved and baptized who were "added to the church" (Acts 2:47).

The command to maintain spirituality in the local church

leads us to the position that the membership must be pure and must live holily, or else it will deteriorate and become carnal (Acts 2:41–47; Titus 2:11–15).

Questions for Study

1. What is the final authority in all our lives and practices?

2. What do we mean when we say the Bible is inspired?

3. What two key words are used to define inspiration? Define them.

4. Mark down 2 Timothy 3:16 and 17 to memorize.

5. Does God seek after man, or man after God, when a man gets saved?

6. Should we ever allow an unsaved person to be a member of a church? Why not?

Chapter 11

MORE ON BAPTIST DISTINCTIVES

I n a day of increasing centralization in power and authority in both the government and the church, our position and conviction on the absolute sovereignty of the local congregation is almost unique in ecclesiastical circles.

The increasing tempo of ecumenism in the liberal camp and the deteriorating lines of doctrinal demarcation in the evangelical ranks will provide an increasing area of challenge and temptation to compromise this historic, Scriptural position.

Sovereign, Independent Local Churches

If you ask the average church member who the final authority in a local church is, you will get a variety of answers: the pastor, the deacons, and so on. Few are convinced and knowledgeable that the congregation is the final authority. No man or group of men or denomination can ever exert its will over a sovereign local church. Its decisions are final. While certain areas of decision making and responsibility can—and ought to be—committed to deacons and other officers, by the constitution and church action, these decisions are always available to the church for scrutiny and veto if deemed necessary. Certainly deacons or pastor/elders do not have the liberty of establishing policy or making decisions beyond local church approval.

A voluntary fellowship between the churches was practiced in the New Testament, and we practice the same today. There is not a hint of suggestion in the Word that justifies the existence of any organization that exercises any control over local churches. To have such would place a human program over a divine institution.

As local New Testament Baptist churches, we are absolutely independent and sovereign in our polity and practice. We should differentiate between the word "independent" and "unaffiliated." All true Bible-following Baptist churches are independent and autonomous. Some independent Baptist churches have voluntarily associated or affiliated themselves together in certain fellowships. In so doing they have not lost their independence. A church in the General Association of Regular Baptist Churches is an independent Baptist church in every sense of the word!

Churches that choose to become a part of no group are also independent Baptists but should be known as "unaffiliated independent Baptists."

There is a term that is perhaps a better one than "independent," and that is the term "interdependent," for while we are certainly independent in polity, we do have a mutual interdependence upon one another in fellowship, outreach, many projects and ministries.

Soul Liberty

Read the following: Acts 5:29; Romans 14:5 and 1 John 2:27.

We believe that every man will give an account of himself before God and that every believer has the Holy Spirit dwelling within him to guide, teach, lead and instruct him.

While recognizing the divine challenge to the local church to maintain certain standards and to keep pride and carnal reactions at a minimum, we believe in the right and freedom of the individual, under the guidance of the Holy Spirit, to read and interpret the Bible as he understands it in his own mind.

A danger is that, with our strong Biblical convictions, we may tend to become intolerant of the *rights* and *beliefs* of others. Our soul liberty does not include such a liberty! As one man said, "Your liberty ends where my nose begins!"

Two Church Offices: Pastor and Deacon

The pastor and deacons are the two officers of the local church found in the Bible. There are no others. They are the spiritual leaders of the church, and there are no other officers over them in that leadership. Thus it is necessary when a church calls and elects a pastor that it give the utmost care in order to provide the church with leadership necessary to keep it Biblical and spiritual. Qualifications for these offices are detailed in 1 Timothy 3.

Other offices—trustee, treasurer, clerk, and the like—are a necessity for the fulfillment of 1 Corinthians 14:40, and the qualifications for these offices should be no less spiritual. However, a church can be a church without them, but it cannot be Scripturally or properly structured without the offices of pastor and deacon. The Bible uses the terms "bishop" and "elder" as further descriptions of the pastor's office—these terms do not refer to offices other than pastor. If you have questions concerning this matter, study passages such as Acts 20:17 and 28 or 1 Peter 5:1 and 2, where all three terms are used synonymously and interchangeably.

Two Ordinances: Baptism and the Lord's Supper

To neglect the observance of these God-given ordinances would be sinful. To invent others or to invest special merit in other church functions would be adding to the Scripture, and Revelation 22:18 specifically warns against such action.

These two ordinances are symbolic of the two basic facets of our relationship to Christ: our *union* with Him as seen in baptism, and our *communion* with Him as seen in the Lord's Table. We have already spent time in chapter 6 studying these ordinances.

Separation of Church and State

This is another Biblical teaching in which Baptists have historically led the way and where many other churches are far from Bible standards.

The *state* is a divinely approved institution to "preserve the rights and liberties of the righteous and to restrain and punish the evil." However, the state includes the unregenerate as well as the regenerate, and God has not given the state the privilege to administer the church, for the church is a body composed of spiritual people.

The *church* is a divine institution designed to evangelize sinners, edify saints and exalt her Savior. Only spiritual people belong in the membership of such a body. Nowhere in the Bible is authority given to the church to exercise any authority over the state.

The breakdown of a clear line of division between the two will bring heartache every time it happens. A church-state or a state-church will result in spiritual depravity and dictatorial powers with invariably accompanying persecution. There is a sad history of lost liberties that accompanies the breakdown of the separation of the church and state.

The Priesthood of All Believers

The priesthood of all believers simply means that every believer has the privilege of worshiping and fellowshipping with the Lord without the aid or interference of another person. No priest or preacher is necessary to lead you into worship. The Old Testament had its priests who interceded for the people. The New Testament (1 Peter 2:9) declares that *we* are a "royal priesthood" and have been granted all the spiritual prerogatives and responsibilities pertaining thereto.

There is a common error in the thinking of some that preachers have a closer tie to God than laymen. This is not so. *Every believer* has priesthood status with instant and open access to the presence of God and should exercise this prerogative regularly.

Conclusion

These nine "distinctives," taken together, mark the Baptists as distinct from other groups and denominations. While some other groups certainly hold to some of these beliefs, the *only true Bible-believing Baptist churches* are those that hold *all* of them.

Carefully examine them again and rejoice at the Scripturality of our position. Then, while holding to these convictions, remember to be a "good Baptist" and allow other brethren their privileges to follow their convictions too—even if they are wrong. Just continue to rejoice in *yours*!

Listing the "distinctives" behind the letters of the word BAPTISTS may help you to remember them. I suggest you memorize them so when someone asks what we believe or how we differ from other churches, you can speak with authority and knowledge, for these are the truths that make Baptists stand out from other denominations. To the best of my knowledge it was my father, Dr. Paul R. Jackson, who first suggested this method of remembering our distinctives. Formerly the national representative of the GARBC, he authored the book, *The Doctrine and Administration of the Church,* which has become a standard on the subject of the church in our schools and churches.

B Baptized, regenerated membership
A Accuracy, authority, inspiration of the Bible
P Priesthood of individual believer
T Two officers: pastor, deacon
I Independent, sovereign local churches
S Sovereignty of God
T Two ordinances: baptism, Lord's Table
S Separation of church and state and soul liberty

Questions for Study

1. Who is the final authority in a local church?

2. What does the word "autonomous" mean relative to church government?

3. Who are the two officers of a local New Testament church mentioned in the Bible, and where are their Scriptural qualifications found?

4. What are the two ordinances of a Baptist church?

5. How involved should the church become in affairs of the state?

DOCTRINE OF FUTURE EVENTS

To reduce the vast subject of the doctrine of future events into a few paragraphs is a superhuman task of condensation and distillation. The scope of subject matter is so great that immense volumes are written on the subject. To interrelate the church, Israel, angels, the unregenerate, the Tribulation saints, the judgments and other future events in two brief lessons is almost impossible. Therefore, this is a brief overview of events that lie ahead for us as revealed in the Bible.

The background of the word "eschatology" gives us the meaning of the study. *Eschatos* means "last, final or future"; and *logos* means "the word" or "teaching." The combination of these two words simply means "the teaching about future things."

In order to get a proper perspective, we need to memorize the following simple timeline:

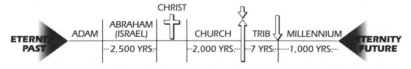

God has always existed. He was never created or had a beginning. He always was. In the Bible, He speaks of His Name as "I Am," indicating His eternal character.

He desired to create a race of men to glorify Himself and to enjoy Him forever. Adam ruined the loveliness of that relationship and brought sin into the race, necessitating a program of regeneration and redemption. For this purpose Israel was called into existence to become the seed line of the coming Messiah King. When He finally came, He was rejected by Israel and crucified.

Now nearly two thousand years have run their course during which time the Lord has been in Heaven at the right hand of the Father. During this time He has been developing the Church—the Bride of Christ—by calling out a people for His name (Acts 15:14). That Bride will soon be translated to Heaven, and the final stages of God's dealing with man will begin.

The Second Coming of Christ is a twofold event beginning with the Rapture and culminating seven years later in the Revelation of Jesus Christ. The Rapture of the Church is the next event in the scheme of things; and believers are to look for it, purify themselves in anticipation of it and wait patiently for it. Every saint, the dead and living, will be instantaneously lifted from earth and into the presence of Christ (1 Thess. 4:16, 17).

We are pretribulational premillennialists; that is, we believe that Christ will return for the saints before the Tribulation period.

This is followed, seven years later, by the Revelation of Jesus Christ, which is the fulfillment of Revelation 19:11, when the Lord shall reign over the earth for one thousand years. It is at this point that He is revealed to the world as the Lord of Glory, and every tongue shall confess and every knee bow to acknowledge Him (Phil. 2:10, 11).

The Great Tribulation falls between these two events and will last for seven years. The terrible judgments spoken of in Revelation 5–18 will be fulfilled during the Tribulation period. It is called "The Time of Jacob's Trouble" and is also referred to as the Seventh Week of Daniel, both terms indicating that the basic character of the period is Jewish; that is, that God will be dealing primarily with Israel during that period.

The millennial (one-thousand-year) reign of Christ will involve the fulfillment of all the promises God made to Abraham and to the other Old Testament saints. It will be a period of peace, prosperity and earth's subjection to Christ, Who will reign in Jerusalem on the throne of David.

There are many other events associated with the subject of future things that need to be placed in perspective. Following are several eschatological features that you will want to study for yourself. Note the chart on page 102.

Events That Will Take Place in Heaven for the Believer Following the Rapture

The Judgment Seat of Believers (1 Cor. 3:11–16; 2 Cor. 5:10)

This judgment will not be a judgment for sin, which was eternally cared for on the cross. It will be a judgment of our works. Some will be there who will receive no rewards as indicated by the phrase in 1 Corinthians 3:15, "saved so as by fire." Others will lose rewards already won (2 John 8). Many will receive great rewards for faithfulness.

The Marriage Supper of the Lamb (Rev. 19:7–9)

This glorious wedding supper will mark the uniting of the Church—the Bride—to the heavenly Bridegroom and will be the fulfillment of all we have hoped and labored for. I believe it will take place in Heaven just prior to our return with Christ.

Return to Earth to Reign with Christ (Rev. 20:6)

At the close of the Tribulation, the Lord will return in great glory (Hab. 2:14; Matt. 25:31) and establish His throne for His one-thousand-year reign on earth. All saints, then glorified, will return with Him to reign.

Events Related to the Tribulation

Removal of the Holy Spirit and Enthroning of the Antichrist (2 Thess. 2:3–10)

Simultaneous with the translation of the Church to Heaven will be the withdrawing of the sin-restraining influence of the Holy Spirit; and with that, the rapid rise of evil and unrighteousness. The man of sin, the Antichrist, controlled and sponsored by Satan, will then be allowed to come forward. He will likely offer a solution to the troubles of the Mideast, make a treaty with Israel, restore their worship and bring about a quasi-peace.

This treaty will be broken halfway through the Tribulation. A time of terror will then be poured out upon the wicked world to the extent that God has stated, "Except those days should be shortened, there should no flesh be saved" (Matt. 24:21, 22).

Character of the Tribulation

Scripture refers to this seven-year period as the "Time of Jacob's Trouble," indicating that although Gentile nations will suffer, too, it is to be a time of God's special dealing with Israel. The very name indicates that it is to be a time of divine judgment.

Israel

This special people, called by God "the apple of his eye," are under judgment for the rejection of their Messiah-King. Judicially Israel was scattered throughout the nations for centuries. The establishment of the new nation of Israel in 1948 may be a significant step in God's plan to restore the nation to its proper homeland.

Though returning there in unbelief, nonetheless the Israelites are coming home. Punished during the Tribulation, they will then recognize their King, acknowledge their terrible error and weep for Him Whom they pierced. A nation will be saved in a day (Isa. 66:8; Zech. 12:9, 10).

All the long-promised blessings made to Abraham thousands of years ago will finally be brought to pass during the Millennium. The Prince of Peace will reign over all the kingdoms of earth, and perfect peace will reign for a thousand years (Isa. 2:2–4). Many people have difficulty in understanding the Scriptures because they attempt to place the fulfillment of the Kingdom promises in our day.

Events Related to the Revelation of Christ

Armageddon

An awful climactic battle will mark the transition from the Tribulation to the Millennium. The armies of earth at least 200 million strong will gather to march against Israel. At that moment Christ will step out of the heavens with all the armies of Heaven, destroy the accumulated armies of earth and establish peace (Rev. 19).

Tribulation Saints

The countless throng saved during the Tribulation, most of whom will have been martyred for their faith, will be raised at the Revelation of Christ (Rev. 20:4).

Satan Put Away

The Devil will be taken by an angel and placed in the bottomless pit for the thousand years of the Millennium. He will then be loosed for a "little season" to deceive the nations prior to being cast into Hell (Rev. 20:3, 7, 8).

Present State of the Dead

During Old Testament times the *saved* who died went into the heart of the earth to a place called Abraham's bosom. They remained there until Christ emptied it at His death and took all their spirits to Heaven. The *unsaved* spirits went into Sheol into punishment and torment and remain there until the present time.

Now, the *unsaved* who die go to the same place, called Hades in the New Testament, and the *saved* who die go immediately into Paradise and the presence of the Lord (Luke 16:19–31; 23:43).

The Resurrections

The unsaved dead from all time past will reside in Hades until the end of the Millennium when they will be brought before the Lord at the Great White Throne Judgment. Their names will not be found in the Lamb's Book of Life, and they will be cast into Hell forevermore (Rev. 20:11–15).

Satan

Original Sin

As part of the original angelic creation, Satan (whose name was Lucifer) was one of the highest ranks of angels. Pride entered his heart, and when he sought to overthrow God's throne, he was thrown out of Heaven accompanied by large numbers of angels who followed his lead and became evil angels (Isa. 14:12–17; Ezek. 28:11–19).

Present Status

His present realm is in the regions above the earth. The Bible calls him the prince of the power of the air (Eph. 2:2). Also known as "the god of this age" and "the god of this world," he is the enemy of Christ and all who name the name of Christ.

His Defeat and Doom

When Christ died on the cross, He forever sealed Satan's doom. The sting of all his threats was forever removed (Heb. 2:14). He roams about "as a roaring lion seeking whom he may devour," although he may appear as an "angel of light." He will ultimately be sealed forever in Hell (1 Pet. 5:8; Rev. 20:10).

The Eternal State

After the Tribulation's dark days, after the peaceful Millennium, after the heavens and earth have been purged by fire, after all unbelief and all enemies of Christ have been delivered to eternal punishment, then the eternal state will begin. The Bible simply says, "And time will be no more."

FROM CALVARY TO ETERNITY

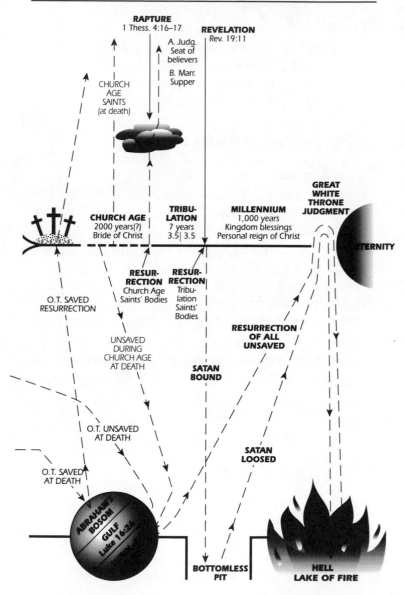

Eternity for every child of God will be a permanent state of blissful service, worship and glory. Throughout all eternity we will be discovering new things about our infinite God. And even eternity will not be long enough!

The study of future events is calculated to stir the heart of the believer to great hope (1 John 3:3) but is sufficiently shrouded in mystery and, to a divinely designed degree, hidden to us so that we do not have all the answers.

Questions for Study

1. What does the word "eschatology" mean?

2. What two events are associated with the return of Jesus Christ?

3. How long will the Tribulation last?

4. How long will the Millennium last?

5. What will the basis of judgment be at the Judgment Seat of believers?

6. Where are the unsaved dead?

7. What is the present place of activity of Satan?

DOCTRINE OF FUTURE EVENTS

Following the Rapture (refer to chart on p. 102), there will be a period of time known as the Tribulation. Some people believe that we are in that time now, but a careful study of the Scriptures will reveal that that period will not begin until the Church and the Holy Spirit are removed from the earth. See 2 Thessalonians 2:7 and 8 and Revelation 3:10.

The Tribulation

The Tribulation period will be seven years long. Daniel 9:24–27 prophetically reveals this fact. Seventy "weeks" are determined "upon Israel" during which all six items mentioned in verse 24 will be fulfilled. Space does not allow us to go into detail on the weeks, but we believe it to be a period of 490 years, 483 of which were fulfilled at the time of Christ. Seven years remain to complete the prophecy. They are the seven years of the Tribulation or the Seventieth Week of Daniel.

For the first half of the Tribulation the Antichrist will make a covenant with Israel (v. 27) and allow them to build their temple and to reestablish their worship, and they will have peace. Then "in the [middle] of the week" (v. 27), Antichrist will break the treaty and usher in what the Spirit describes in

Daniel 12:1 and Matthew 24:21 as the "Great Tribulation." It is this last half of the Tribulation that is prophetically revealed to be forty-two months in length (Rev. 13:5). It is also called "a time, times, and an half" in Daniel 12:7, and 1,290 days in Daniel 12:11 and 12. (See Scofield Bible note on Daniel 12.)

69 WEEKS		CHURCH AGE		TRIBULATION 1 WEEK		MILLENNIAL KINGDOM
483 YRS. FULFILLED		PAUSE		7 YRS. YET UNFULFILLED		1,000 years

The Antichrist will head up a coalition of syncretized religion during the Tribulation and lead it into subjection to the world ruler so that a one-world government and one-world religion will become a fact.

It is interesting to see the framework for both areas of such future events already shaping up now. The United Nations looks toward the day of world peace under their control. The National Council of Churches and World Council of Churches are pushing ecumenicalism and are now in dialogue with Romanism and other so-called religious bodies, moving toward a world church.

Only two things are lacking: (1) the removal of the true Church, and (2) the raising up of the international leaders who might even now be in the news and merely waiting for the proper moment and the necessary removal of the Body of Christ to take their place! Surely these are the last hours of the age.

The Millennium

Matthew 24:15–31 gives a picture of the transitional events that will mark the close of the Tribulation and the return of Christ. Revelation 19:11 paints a graphic picture of the sudden return of Jesus Christ to earth.

While the Tribulation marks a period of national chastisement for Israel, the Millennium will be the time of her blessing.

The curse placed upon the earth in Adam's time will be removed, prosperity will arrive, peace will reign and Christ will be present on earth ruling as King of Kings in Jerusalem. For a thousand years the world will know peace and perfect righ-teousness (Isa. 2:4).

The saints of the Church Age are told that we shall "reign with him" during this time. Apparently the position and place of responsibility will be in direct proportion to our faithfulness and loyalty to Christ now (Rev. 20:4).

Final Judgment

At the close of the one-thousand-year reign, Satan who will have been bound and cast into the bottomless pit at the return of Christ (Rev. 20:1, 2), will be loosed and will go about deceiving many. For though all will be saved who enter into the Millennium, many will be born during those years who evidently will not receive Christ in spite of the fact that He is here personally. Many of these Satan will lead to himself and on to Hell (Rev. 20:8).

This will be the final, conclusive evidence that the natural heart of man is deceitful, wicked and at enmity with God.

The Great White Throne Judgment, described in Revelation 20:11, will be the place to which all the unregenerate dead of all the ages and all the unsaved of the final age will be brought for judgment. Their names not being found in the Lamb's Book of Life, they will be cast into Hell with the Devil and his angels for ever and ever (Rev. 20:11–15).

All Things New

The last two chapters of Revelation are descriptions of future events that give the skeptic something to scoff about, for they seem so improbable of fulfillment. But they offer the believer cause for rejoicing. What wonderful things are in store for us! What delightful wonders await their fulfillment in the eternity that lies ahead!

It behooves us to be about the Father's business and to abide in Christ. The time is so short, the unbelievers so numerous, the Church so asleep! Let us awake, arise and obey His command, "Occupy *till I come!*"

BOOK LIST

Recommended for Reading and Acquistion

Many of the books on this list are available at almost any Christian bookstore. Some (marked with *) may be secured from Regular Baptist Press, 1300 N. Meacham Road, Schaumburg, Illinois 60173–4888. Unfortunately some are now no longer in print and will have to be found in libraries or used bookstores.

Practical Reading

Ketcham, Robert T. *God's Provision for Normal Christian Living*. Schaumburg, IL: Regular Baptist Press, 1977.

LaHaye, Tim. *The Spirit-Controlled Temperament*. Wheaton, IL: Tyndale House Publishers, 1979.

LaHaye, Tim. *Transformed Temperaments*. Wheaton, IL: Tyndale House Publishers, 1979.

Theological

Bancroft, Emery. *Elemental Theology*. Grand Rapids: Zondervan Publishing House, 1960.

*Jackson, Paul R. *Doctrine and Administration of the Church*. Schaumburg, IL: Regular Baptist Press, 1989.

Lightner, Robert. *Church Union—A Layman's Guide*. Schaumburg, IL: Regular Baptist Press, 1971.

Packer, J. I. *Knowing God*. Downers Grove, IL: InterVarsity Press, 1979.

Missionary

Hopewell, William. *Missionary Emphasis of the GARBC*. Schaumburg, IL: Regular Baptist Press, 1963.

*Matthews, R. L. *Missionary Administration in the Local Church*. Schaumburg, IL: Regular Baptist Press, 1976.

Olsen, Viggo. *Daktar*. Chicago: Moody Press, 1973.

Book Study

Baxter, J. Sidlow. *Explore the Book*. Grand Rapids: Zondervan Publishing House, 1979.

Henry, Matthew. *Matthew Henry's Commentary on the Whole Bible*. Grand Rapids: Zondervan Publishing House, 1979.

Jamieson, R., A. R. Fausset and Brown. *Jamieson, Fausset and Brown's Commentary on the Whole Bible*. Grand Rapids: Zondervan Publishing House, 1979.

Prophetic

McClain, Alva. *The Greatness of the Kingdom.* Winona Lake, IN: BMH Books, 1979.

Pentecost, Dwight. *Things to Come.* Grand Rapids: Zondervan Publishing House, 1979.

Walvoord, John F. *The Revelation of Jesus Christ.* Chicago: Moody Press, 1966.

Family Help

Dobson, James. *Dare to Discipline.* Wheaton, IL: Tyndale House Publishers, 1977.

McDonald, Cleveland. *Creating a Successful Christian Marriage.* Grand Rapids: Baker Book House, 1975.

Charts

Larkin, Clarence. *Dispensational Truth.* Clarence Larkin Estate, 1918.

Bible Dictionary

Wycliffe Historical Geography of Bible Lands. Chicago: Moody Press, 1979.

Unger, Merrill F. *Unger's Bible Dictionary.* Chicago: Moody Press, 1979.

Bible Translations

Wuest, Kenneth S., ed. *New American Standard Bible.* Anaheim, CA: Foundation Publications, 1970.

_____. *New International Version.* Grand Rapids: Zondervan Publishing House, 1978.

History

Kuiper, B. K. *The Church in History.* Grand Rapids: Wm. B. Eerdmans Publishing Company, 1953.

Vedder, H. C. *Short History of the Baptists.* Philadelphia: American Baptist Publication Society, 1907.

Biography

*Murdoch, J. Murray. *Portrait of Obedience: The Biography of Robert T. Ketcham.* Schaumburg, IL: Regular Baptist Press, 1986.